FLORIDA STATE DEVOTIONS

INSPIRATIONAL STORIES FOR THE 'NOLE NATION

DEL DUDUIT

ANDY CLAPP

BETHANY JETT

IRON
STREAM
Birmingham, Alabama

Florida State Devotions

Iron Stream
An imprint of Iron Stream Media
100 Missionary Ridge
Birmingham, AL 35242
IronStreamMedia.com

Library of Congress Control Number: 2022939444

Cover design by Jonathan Lewis / Jonlin Creative

ISBN: 978-1-56309-601-3 (paperback)
ISBN: 978-1-56309-602-0 (eBook)

1 2 3 4 5—26 25 24 23 22

This book is dedicated to my friends and colleagues with
Serious Writer, Inc. You all know who you are.
Cyle, Patty, Bethany, Michelle, Brit, Andy, Julie, and Angie.
—*Del*

In memory of Bobby Bowden—he granted me an interview
when I was starting as a writer and shared the story of his faith,
which stoked my passion for my faith.
—*Andy*

To my dad, for taking me to my first Seminole football game.
To Nathaniel, for carrying the torch of 'Nole Nation diehardness.
To the amazing people of FSU's Christian Campus Fellowship
(CCF), for making my college experience feel like home.
And to all those blessed enough to call themselves
Florida State Seminoles, for we are *unconquered.*
—*Bethany*

CONTENTS

ACKNOWLEDGMENTS

FROM DEL

Several people played key roles in making this book a reality. I would like to thank the following for their efforts in bringing this book to you.

- ➤ My wife, Angie, for being the initial editor of this book and for her support.

- ➤ My agent, Cyle Young, for his work to get my work in front of the right people.

- ➤ My coauthors Bethany Jett and Andy Clapp for your friendships.

- ➤ My publisher, John Herring, for his trust and faith in me.

- ➤ My editors Larry J. Leech II and Susan Cornell for making this product better.

- ➤ The production crew at Iron Stream Media.

- ➤ My Lord and Savior for this exciting opportunity.

FROM ANDY

I would like to thank my coauthors, Del Duduit and Bethany Jett, for allowing me to be part of this project. To work with my friends was an absolute blessing. I would also like to thank Iron Stream Media for this opportunity and for believing in us.

I also thank my agent, Cyle Young, as I would not be where I am without him. Thank you for all you do. I am eternally thankful to the Lord for every door He opens and for giving me the chance to spread the gospel in so many ways. My wife and children also deserve so much credit as they understand when I spend late nights writing.

Thank you to my church, Mt. Zion Baptist Church of Liberty, NC, for your unwavering support of all I do and for your commitment to reach the world for Jesus. Thank you to my parents and all of my family. I also want to thank Mark Richt, who gave me an interview many years ago and shared about Bobby Bowden's impact on his life.

Thank you to all my friends who keep me going in life. Your support pushes me to strive even harder to become who God has called me to be. I cannot list all of you, but all of you know who you are.

FROM BETHANY

Writing may often feel like a solitary endeavor but there are so many people involved in the publishing process. My biggest thanks to the following people:

Justin, Jeremy, Jedidiah, and Josiah—You are the four loves of my life. Even though at least two of you have chosen a team on the dark side, I forgive you. #HouseDivided

Del Duduit, one of my coauthors—Truly, you made writing this book a reality for me. I've loved Florida State for so many years, so to be part of your sports series is an absolute honor. Thank you from the bottom of my garnet-and-gold heart.

Andy Clapp, my other coauthor—Thanks for bringing so much enthusiasm to this project. It's so fun with you onboard, and I'm so happy that we have a book together!

Acknowledgments

Cyle Young, my agent—Thanks for your help coordinating all the moving parts. Here's hoping for an FSU vs. U-M championship game in the near future.

The team at Iron Stream Media—Holding this book is a dream come true and it wouldn't be possible without you. Thank you so much!

My dad, Dr. Jeffery Donley—Thank you so much for taking me to that football game oh-so-many years ago. I walked in cheering for Notre Dame and came out a true FSU believer. That game was life-changing in many ways. Thank you from the bottom of my heart.

My brother, Nathaniel Donley—You'll never know how much it means that you love Florida State as much as I do. I love that we share this passion and I'm so glad you're my brother. I love you so much.

My sister, Jill Lancour—I forgive you for putting Presley in the Gator cheer uniform. We'll pretend it was Halloween. Love you so much.

My mom, Johnnie Alexander, and heart-sister Natalie Snodgrass—One of my fave memories is our FSU game together with Jill. I love you both so much and, Natalie, SO glad you're all-in with the garnet and gold too! Yasssss!

Ashley Seal—*Dahling!* I am SO proud of you for completing our collective dream and actually earning a Florida State diploma. You are one of my heroes and I love you so much. And, Jason, someday, you'll see the light. I'm sure of it!

Susan, my mentor at FSU's Christian Campus Fellowship— You had such an impact on my spiritual life and journey. I am FOREVER grateful.

The entire CCF group, as well as Matt, Adam, Clint, Amy, Kyle, Ashley, Shannon, Buddy, and Mike (and his beautiful wife,

Shannon)—thanks for being my friend during our time at FSU. Even though it was short-lived for me, I'm grateful to have such great memories, so thank you.

And finally, to all those who cheer along with me on social media during FSU wins and mourn with the losses, thanks for the camaraderie. This book is for you.

DAY 1
DON'T BLOCK GOD'S BLESSINGS

October 8, 2016: Florida State 20, Miami 19
By Del Duduit

Every good gift and every perfect gift is from above, coming down from the Father of lights with whom there is no variation or shadow due to change. —James 1:17

The Miami Hurricanes, ranked No. 10 in the nation, had just put themselves in a position to tie the game with twenty-third-ranked Florida State.

Quarterback Brad Kaaya found receiver Stacy Coley on an 11-yard touchdown pass to close the gap to 1 point with under two minutes to play in the game at Hard Rock Stadium in Miami. Kicker Michael Badgley entered the game having made 72 consecutive extra points, and this appeared to be another chip shot to send the game into overtime.

But Seminole's defensive end DeMarcus Walker had other ideas.

The 6'3" Walker blasted through the offensive line and stretched his long arms high enough to block the extra point attempt that would have tied the game at 20.

The 'Noles came back in the second half thanks in part to touchdown catches from running back Dalvin Cook and receiver Kermit Whitfield.

FSU quarterback Deondre Francois returned in the second half after an injury sidelined him earlier in the game. He finished the game with 234 yards passing.

Cook, who rushed for 150 yards on the ground, gave FSU a big lift when he made a 59-yard TD reception. Then, Whitfield's 20-yard touchdown catch put the team ahead for good.

But in the end, Walker's block saved the win for the Seminoles.

> But if God so clothes the grass of the field, which today is alive and tomorrow is thrown into the oven, will he not much more clothe you, O you of little faith? Therefore do not be anxious, saying, "What shall we eat?" or "What shall we drink?" or "What shall we wear?" For the Gentiles seek after all these things, and your heavenly Father knows that you need them all. But seek first the kingdom of God and his righteousness, and all these things will be added to you. —Matthew 6:30–33

God loves to bless His children, and you should be thankful for all the many ways he blesses you daily. But if you're not careful, you can block them from happening.

FEAR THE SPEAR

God is your provider. Everything you possess is because of Him. Christ is generous and wants the best for you. But do you always acknowledge His gifts to you? Or are you always looking at others with envy and complaining about what they have that you don't have? Perhaps you thought you should have received a promotion at work, and it went to someone else. Are you grateful that you still have a job and truly happy for the person who was selected? Or do you focus on your problems and pout about not being selected yourself?

'NOLE NATION

God's blessings might not always come in the form or fashion you think they should. Maybe you have decided how you think he should bless you, but he chooses something different and innovative to answer your prayer.

Recognize the fundamental things in life as kisses from God. Life. Safety and protection. Health. A sound mind. Family. Friends. Freedom. Church. And on and on the list could go. Don't get so busy in this fast-paced world that you fail to notice how much God freely blesses you every day. Here are some ways that you might be blocking the great things God has in store for you.

1. Pride: This can get in the way of many blessings. If you complain about your job long enough without giving thanks to God for it, you might just lose it. If you put other things ahead of His plans for your life, you might lose them too. God wants to be your priority. Block out the pride, and let humility and gratitude take over for the score. "For though the LORD is high, he regards the lowly, but the haughty he knows from afar" (Psalm 138:6).

2. A negative attitude: If you have a negative and pessimistic mindset, you might block the opportunities God gives you and justify your resistance. You are either too scared or too lazy to walk through the doors the Master opens for you. Don't get stuck and quit

moving forward, and don't fear failure. Keep in mind that the devil will throw every interception he can to try to stop your progress. If God cracks the door, open it with prayer and faith. A positive attitude of trust in what God has for you is always best. "A joyful heart is good medicine, but a crushed spirit dries up the bones" (Proverbs 17:22).

3. You are bitter: No kicker will put the ball through the uprights as long as bitterness stands in the way. Unforgiveness can be a huge hindrance to fully receiving God's blessings on your life. When bitterness festers and grows inside you, it steals your joy and your peace. If you want to experience the grace and love the Lord has for you, then you must forgive and toss bitterness out of bounds.

4. You resist the Holy Spirit: When you run from God's calling on your life, then you block His blessings. If you are obedient to His direction in your life, He will bless you. God may be calling you into a ministry—such as a pastor or missionary—or his call might be to be of service to others. Either way, you experience true freedom when you answer His call upon your life. God may call you to fill a role behind the scenes, such as serving food at a homeless shelter, or he may expect you to serve in a very public position, such as a pastor. Either way, a calling doesn't have to be something where you are visibly seen and appreciated for the work you have done. If He asks you to take a leap of faith, then trust Him. God will honor your obedience.

5. You are lazy: God will not bless you if you are not willing to work. Take time each day to read the Word and pray. Make it a priority to attend the House of God on a regular basis. Go to extra services or revivals when you can. Tell others about His goodness. Donate your time to worthy causes and help those in need. Would a coach put you into the game if you never practiced? Put in the time. "A slack hand causes poverty, but the hand of the diligent makes rich" (Proverbs 10:4).

Walker's block saved the season for the Seminoles. The team finished 10-3 and ranked No. 8. His play was positive for FSU, and the timing of your plays will influence your future success as a Christian. Watch out for the tackles and trick plays and focus on the score. You want to experience the joy of the Lord on every down and every day.

DAY 2
SETTING A NEW STANDARD

January 1, 1988: Florida State 31, Nebraska 28
By Andy Clapp

Jesus Christ is the same yesterday, today, and forever.
—Hebrews 13:8 HCSB

Bobby Bowden sought to build a powerhouse program.

Two top-ten finishes in the final Associated Press poll in 1979 and 1980 showed glimpses of what could be, but the following six seasons were marked with at least three losses each season.

As they entered the 1988 Fiesta Bowl, the 'Noles were ranked third, facing off against fifth-ranked Nebraska. The test opened the door for the Seminoles to make a statement to the college football world.

Nebraska dominated the first quarter, racing out to a 14-0 lead. Then, the momentum shifted to FSU as the 'Noles owned the second quarter, scoring 21 unanswered points to enter the halftime locker room with a 21-14 lead.

As the Cornhuskers reclaimed the lead, Nebraska drove the field in the fourth quarter to put the game away. Leading 28-24, Tom Osborne's team lined up at the two-yard line to punch in a potentially devastating score. Tyreese Knox took the handoff and launched himself over the pile.

The 'Noles defense, however, met him in midair, jarring the ball loose and recovering the fumble to give the offense one last chance.

Danny McManus led FSU on a march toward the end zone. Facing fourth and goal from the fifteen, McManus hit Ronald Lewis in the end zone to cap a 97-yard drive.

The win served as a springboard. FSU finished second in the nation, beginning their streak of fourteen straight years finishing in the top five in the nation.

The 'Noles became the powerhouse program Bowden dreamed it would be, serving as a model to other programs longing to reach the top. Their consistency continued their domination that began on the first day of January in Tempe, Arizona.

> Therefore, my dear brothers, be steadfast, immovable, always excelling in the Lord's work, knowing that you labor in the Lord is not in vain. —1 Corinthians 15:58 HCSB

FEAR THE SPEAR

You have dreams of rising higher in your life. What you envision is not where you are right now, but today, you can take a step toward the goal. You look at others and see their accomplishments, then look at your own life and feel the desperation of not accomplishing what you set out to do. Previous years have perhaps contained a series of inconsistencies, the rollercoaster of a season on top followed by deep descents into the valley. Now is the time to reach the top and set a new standard for yourself and your life. You can do it. You need to do it. As we live in the most inconsistent times, you have the chance to set the precedence by living differently.

'NOLE NATION

Take the step today. What is at your disposal today is the opportunity and your attitude. From today, your follow-up dictates the outcome. As believers, we are called to follow Christ, to take on more of His nature in our lives. Two scriptures that push us to rise to the top are found in the New Testament.

In Mark, he captured the reactions of the people to what they saw in Jesus. Christ left a mark on those He encountered. Mark wrote, "They were extremely astonished and said, 'He has done everything well! He even makes deaf people hear, and people unable to speak, talk'" (Mark 7:37 HCSB). Christ did everything well. What He did captivated those around Him. The same should be seen in our lives.

The second verse comes from Hebrews 13:8. The writer of Hebrews pointed out the consistency in the life of Jesus. He remains the same. Conditions change in our lives, and situations shift without notice. But Jesus remains the same. Consistency marks the life of a committed follower of Christ. For the sake of righteousness, keep this phrase in your head—"Do it well, and do that always." Consistency leads us to a life of better results and a better reflection of Jesus throughout every day of our lives.

Everything needs a starting point. So, here is where you can get started today building a dynasty in your life:

1. Forget failures—those who focus only on the missed opportunities of yesterday miss the opportunity of today. Previous seasons of life led to where you are now, and growth resulted from those earlier failures.

2. Win in the small things—life has guaranteed wins. There are easy victories to be had today, whether it be helping prepare dinner tonight, taking out the garbage, or calling a friend to check on them. Small victories daily lead to dynasty building.

3. Pray—ask the Lord to reveal the opportunities before you today. He sees the ones that we often overlook. Pray that He opens your eyes to see what He's placed before you.

4. Choose faith, let go of fear—Big moments challenge us to have big faith. Building a dynasty in life and faith never comes from remaining comfortable. Seize the chance to fly higher today.

5. Follow it up tomorrow—the consistent person is an effective person. As you give today your all, do the same tomorrow. Take the initiative to build tomorrow on what you started today.

The run of the 'Noles for fourteen seasons inspired other programs to aspire to reach the same level. As you set a consistent standard in your life, others will be inspired by you.

DAY 3
TAKE THE RISK

November 17, 1988: FSU 24, Clemson 21
By Bethany Jett

Behold, I am doing a new thing; now it springs forth,
do you not perceive it? I will make a way in the wilderness and rivers in the desert. —Isaiah 43:19

The Seminoles were tied with Clemson in the fourth quarter
with only a couple of minutes to go. With Florida State fourth
and four at their 21-yard line, Coach Bobby Bowden threw
caution to the wind.

Time to call the play they'd practiced but never performed
in a game. "'I had been thinking of it through the last three
series we ran,' he said. 'But it hadn't worked out just right to set
it up. Actually, I had thought about it the whole game.'"[1]

The play was the Puntrooskie, aka "The Rooskie," a fake
punt.

"Down. Set. Hike." The ball shoots through the center's legs
into the hands of fullback Dayne Williams, who took off to the
right, but not before he sneakily handed the ball to defensive
back LeRoy Butler.

---

[1] "1988 Football—Year in Review," https://nolefan.org/summary/
f1988.html.

Clemson took off after Williams while Butler darted to the left. Confusion mounted momentarily until a collective wave of recognition washes across the stadium.

Butler ran 78 yards before a Tiger tackled him just shy of a touchdown. Now at the 1-yard line, Richie Andrews kicked the winning field goal with thirty-two seconds left. And with that, the 'Noles cemented another innovative play that lives on in FSU infamy.

> He who observes the wind will not sow, and he who regards the clouds will not reap. As you do not know the way the spirit comes to the bones in the womb of a woman with child, so you do not know the work of God who makes everything. In the morning sow your seed, and at evening withhold not your hand, for you do not know which will prosper, this or that, or whether both alike will be good. —Ecclesiastes 11:4–6

FEAR THE SPEAR

The "Rooskie" was one of those new, never-seen-before plays in college football history that still get mentioned when reminiscing over the best plays of our favorite teams. Sometimes the coach calls a play that we haven't practiced a lot, much less tried in real life with thousands of eyes watching. Sometimes God calls us to do something that we're not prepared for either.

Sometimes we have to take a risk.

The Bible is full of such miracles and wonders, including when God parted the Red Sea. Who had ever seen the like?

The Puntrooskie took the opponent by surprise, giving the 'Noles a chance to get ahead. I'd gather that witnessing an entire body of water being separated into walls of H_2O was quite a shock to the Egyptians (and probably the Israelites as well!). But God called, and the people crossed on dry ground to safety before the hands of God moved from the walls of water to bring it crashing down on the enemy.

What if the Israelites had been afraid to move? What if they had been scared to be led into the unknown?

'NOLE NATION

When God calls us, we have to be ready, no matter how big the opposition, no matter how many people are watching. Here are five ways we can be ready:

1. Confirm that God has called you. While we may never be 100 percent sure, we can hear God's voice through prayer, in our circumstances, and from the wisdom of other Christians in our lives who have our best interest at heart.

2. Wait for the opportune moment. When God calls us, we need to be ready to go, but sometimes there is preparation that needs to happen. Move quickly so you don't miss your moment.

3. Trust in your support system. When we're called to move, sometimes it means that we're out in front by ourselves. We have to trust that our support team of family and friends is also listening to God's call for their lives so that we can work in harmony.

Del Duduit, Andy Clapp, and Bethany Jett

4. Run like you've never run before. When you know God is leading you, follow with all your might. Don't hesitate. Don't look back. Run toward the goal.

5. Get ready to do it again. There are many moments that God has planned for us. Once we've started down the path, we have to keep going, ready and waiting for the next play He's going to call.

If we can learn anything, we can learn this: When God is doing big things, we have to be ready to follow His leading.

DAY 4
OVERCOMING GIANTS

September 28, 1991: FSU 51, Michigan 31
By Bethany Jett

For everyone born of God overcomes the world. This is
the victory that has overcome the world, even our faith.
—1 John 5:4

Perennial powerhouse University of Michigan didn't expect
Florida State University to be the only team to crush them,
especially with the Ann Arbor home-field advantage. The last
time the Seminoles and the Wolverines met in 1986, the Ann
Arbor team won. There was no reason to expect anything
different this time.

Florida State came into its fourth game of the season with a
less-than-stellar kicking game, so the best chance at success was
to play to their strengths and protect their weaknesses.

Enter Bobby Bowden with what he called the Crocodile
play. Fun fact: Rumor had it that the 'Noles wouldn't run a play
named after their rival, so instead of the play being called "the
Gator," it was dubbed the Crocodile.

With the score tied at 7, FSU begins with a forward lateral
from Casey Weldon to Charlie Ward, who pitched it back to
Weldon. Protected by the offensive line, Weldon ran 29 yards,
setting the Seminoles up for success.

Four plays later, the 'Noles lined up, faked a field goal, and William Floyd ran 4 yards for a touchdown.

The two successful plays allowed Florida State to keep its less-than-stellar kicking game in check while out-maneuvering the other team to victory.

When the last second ticked off the play clock in the fourth quarter, the score was 51-31 in the Seminoles' favor. This win marked a significant moment in Michigan football history, with the 'Noles scoring the greatest number of points against the Wolverines on their home field.

> Then David said to the Philistine, "You come to me with a sword and with a spear and with a javelin, but I come to you in the name of the LORD of hosts, the God of the armies of Israel, whom you have defied. This day the LORD will deliver you into my hand, and I will strike you down and cut off your head . . . the LORD saves not with sword and spear. For the battle is the LORD's, and he will give you into our hand." —1 Samuel 17:45, 47

FEAR THE SPEAR

Probably the greatest story in the Scriptures about playing to your strengths is the story of the matchup between the giant Goliath and the underdog David the shepherd.

When David went up against Goliath, he didn't try to use the latest and greatest in warfare. He didn't choose hand-to-hand combat. Instead, David played to his strengths. As a shepherd, he was fast, strong, and had lots of practice time to shoot rocks and stones with his sling.

David's strength wasn't in close-up battle. It was striking a target from a distance. And that's what God used to help David defeat the giant who threatened His people. God will use your strengths to further His purpose too.

'NOLE NATION

When we feel like we're up against insurmountable odds, we must remember that our God owns the cattle on a thousand hills. He is the God of all creation, and He is there for us when we need him. Here are five ways we can overcome our own giants:

1. Lean into your strengths. What are the talents God has given to you? If you're not sure, ask the people who love you to identify the areas in which you excel.

2. Fill in your weakness. What steps can you take to overcome the areas you're not strong in? Who do you know that can stand in the gap for you?

3. Seek wise counsel. When the chips are down, it can be difficult to see the silver lining or know how we're going to make it through. Find a community, either in person—like at church or a small group—or online. There are lots of faith-based groups that can offer support and encouragement.

4. Have a plan. If you can anticipate where your weak areas are or identify what could go wrong, you can come up with a plan for either how to prevent the undesirable outcome or how to prepare for it when it does.

Del Duduit, Andy Clapp, and Bethany Jett

5. Remember that it is through God's power, not ours, that His will is done. When we celebrate a victory, we must remember that it is God's power and that we do everything for His glory.

Being a powerhouse doesn't mean we're indestructible, but with God, all things are possible.

DAY 5
HOW DO YOU RESPOND?

October 10, 1992: Florida State 36, North Carolina 13
By Andy Clapp

Though a righteous man falls seven times, he will get up, but the wicked will stumble into ruin. —Proverbs 24:16 HCSB

History repeated itself.

In 1991, Wide Right I dashed the hopes of the 'Nole Nation. Florida State followed up the heartbreaking defeat with a loss to Florida to close out the '91 regular season.

In 1992, Wide Right II shook the Seminoles. How would they respond this time?

The answer came quickly. The 'Noles took the opening possession and drove the field. Sean Jackson capped the drive with a 1-yard touchdown run. Kicker Dan Mowery struggled again and missed the extra point, but the miss would be moot at the end of the game. The 'Noles smelled blood from the beginning and went in for the early kill.

Mickey Andrews's defense smothered the Tar Heels on the initial drive. A quick three-and-out forced Carolina to punt to the always dangerous Corey Sawyer.

Thomas boomed the kick down the field. Sawyer faced a sea of light blue but refused to call for a fair catch. Instead, he fielded the punt, stared down four Tar Heels, then cut to his

19

left and accelerated, leaving the four grasping at air. Dancing down the sideline, he cut toward the middle of the field for a moment, avoided the punter, and jetted to the end zone.

Carolina managed to pull within six but no closer. The 'Noles refused to allow the previous week's disappointment to derail their dreams. Nothing could change the loss to Miami, but focusing on that loss could have been lethal when facing North Carolina. When the final whistle blew, the blowout propelled FSU forward in pursuit of another great season that ended with a ranking in the top five of college football.

> But one thing I do: Forgetting what is behind and reaching forward to what is ahead, I pursue as my goal the prize promised by God's heavenly call in Christ Jesus. —Philippians 3:13–14 HCSB

FEAR THE SPEAR

The setbacks of yesterday can leave you stunned. If we aren't careful, one setback freezes us in place or sends us careening in the wrong direction. You replay the stumble over and over again, thinking only about what might have been if the outcome was different. Time escapes as we fail to shake off what cannot be changed to take control of what can be controlled. One setback can ruin an entire season of your existence, can ruin a life totally, or can simply be a setback along the way. After a fall, what dictates our future is our determination to get back up.

'NOLE NATION

Proverbs 24:16 talks about the response of both the righteous and the wicked when a setback occurs. What does it tell us?

How Do You Respond?

Everyone stumbles in life. Even with our best efforts, we fall at times. Those falls threaten to define us as we fear what others might think. But the mistakes, the shortcomings, and the stumbles along the way are not what tell the story. How we respond to them is what tells the true story.

Proverbs says the righteous get back up. Regardless of how many times they fall, they brush themselves off, returning to the pursuit of the Lord, recognizing that there is more to be done.

What if Peter had given up when his walk on the water ended in a near-drowning? So many lives would have been negatively impacted if Peter had abandoned the call when a stumble occurred. Could you imagine if Moses quit on life after his sin of killing an Egyptian became known to others? So much of the story of the children of Israel would have been affected if Moses had run away and never come back. Throughout the Bible, the Lord repeatedly chose to use people who had previously failed.

The greatest hero stories feature an aspect of overcoming because all of us have obstacles to overcome. The sting of failure hurts for a moment, but ultimately, it drives a champion to be even better in the aftermath. So, what steps can we take to respond correctly after a fall in life? Here are a few ideas:

1. Keep failure in perspective—every person falls at some point. When we think we are the only ones to stumble in such a way, we must remember that none of us are perfect. Don't compare your fall with others, but at the same time, don't overreact to the fall either.

2. Learn from the fall—look back, even as painful as it may be, and see what can be learned from the mistake. Devise

a plan from what you have learned to avoid a repeat fall in the same area later in life.

3. Remember redemption in your response—the cross bore all our sins, every shortcoming in our lives. The cross reminds us that Christ took care of the fall, that He paid the price for our sins, and did so completely.

4. See that there is work yet to be done—the season is not over. There remains work to be done. Focus on what can be done rather than on what cannot be changed.

5. Give yourself some grace—just as the Lord gives us grace, we must give ourselves some grace from time to time.

The 'Noles refocused after the setback against Miami because there was still much to play for in the 1992 season. Their response reminds us that we can dust ourselves off and claim victory even after a disappointing fall in life.

DAY 6
DON'T BE SATISFIED

January 2, 1997: Florida 52, Florida State 20
By Del Duduit

But grow in the grace and knowledge of our Lord and
Savior Jesus Christ. To him be the glory both now and
to the day of eternity. Amen. —2 Peter 3:18

What goes around comes around.

On November 30, 1996, Florida State knocked off Florida,
24-21. The FSU defense harassed and chased Gator QB Danny
Wuerffel all night long. He was sacked six times and smacked
around like a piñata.

Although Florida lost that game, Coach Steve Spurrier
learned a huge lesson and made some needed adjustments for
their next matchup.

The two teams did meet again—for the college national
championship in the Nokia Sugar Bowl at the Superdome in
New Orleans, Louisiana.

The Seminoles took the opening drive and marched down
to the Florida 23-yard line, thanks in part to a well-timed
33-yard pass from quarterback Thad Busby to receiver Andre
Cooper. Florida State Coach Bobby Bowden opted to go for it
on fourth-and-one instead of kicking a field goal.

The Gators chomped down and stuffed the play.

That gave Florida momentum, and Wuerffel used the newly installed shotgun to perfection. He led a 77-yard drive and completed five passes which included a nine-yard TD strike to Ike Hilliard for the early lead.

In the second quarter, Wuerffel led the Gators 73 yards in under thirty seconds to boost the lead to 17-3.

The Seminoles answered when Warrick Dunn capped off a 66-yard drive with a 12-yard romp into the end zone to cut the deficit to 24-17.

But the Gators used the shotgun throughout the second half and outscored FSU 28-3 in the final two quarters.

Wuerffel was named the MVP of the game. He threw for 306 yards and three touchdowns and ran for one to lead the Gators to the championship.

"Now do you see why we didn't want to play them again?" Bowden said after the game.

Spurrier learned from the loss and made key adjustments while FSU was content with the way things were and lost.

As a believer, never be content to stay in a rut. You should always strive to get closer to God and bring others into the kingdom. Go deeper in the Word and increase your prayer life to prepare you for bigger and better things in your walk with Christ.

> Practice these things, immerse yourself in them, so that all may see your progress. —1 Timothy 4:15

FEAR THE SPEAR

Maybe you professed your love for the Lord a few years back and you feel good about your life. You don't have any real complaints or issues. You go to church when you feel like it and read your Bible once in a while. Your prayer life is OK, but it could be better. You might even believe that it can be overrated at times. Since you don't have any real problems and life is going at a nice pace, you may not feel the need to be close to God as you could be. All your needs are met. Your job is good. You have all the luxuries you believe you need. But what happens when your world gets sacked? Have you made preparations for the unexpected, or are you content with keeping Christ at a distance?

'NOLE NATION

Bowden did not make any changes to his defense because it worked the first time the Seminoles played Florida and won. But Spurrier noticed that something needed to change. His QB needed more time to throw, and the shotgun paid off. What changes in your life have you made to deal with adversity? How strong is your faith? Are you growing in the Lord, or are you staying in the same place you were in when you got saved? Here are some tips for moving forward as a Christian.

1. Spread the Word: You don't hesitate to tell your friends about your favorite sports team and the details of their latest victory. Many of you can't wait to announce good news on social media. You should also share the news of Jesus Christ and God's love. You don't have to bombard people every day and come across as a person others might want to avoid. But mix in some posts about a great message you heard at church or how touched your heart was by a gospel song. You can also post an encouraging verse from the Bible now and then. The point here is to

let others know how good Christ has been to you. You will find this will help you grow: "and I pray that the sharing of your faith may become effective for the full knowledge of every good thing that is in us for the sake of Christ" (Philemon 1:6).

2. Exercise: Just as players need to be fit mentally and physically for each game, you too need to be strong in the Lord. If you don't practice your faith, it will become weak. When you attend church consistently, pray, and read your Bible daily, you will notice how much stronger you will become. Be sure to carve out time each day for your spiritual workouts.

3. Prepare: This one is similar to the second point, but it's crucial to spend time in prayer and in worship to the Lord. No coach will take his team into a game without proper practice and preparation. You must spend time in the Word and in communication with the Master. This is the only way to know the playbook of life. When you spend time with Jesus, your faith in Him will increase. "And rising very early in the morning, while it was still dark, he departed and went out to a desolate place, and there he prayed" (Mark 1:35).

4. Pray and meditate: When you read a passage of scripture, don't just read it to check the box. Take time to understand what God is telling you. If you run into complications and don't comprehend what happened, then go further in the Word and obtain a concordance or a Bible that goes into detail to explain what took place and what it means. It will renew your mind and cause your faith to grow.

5. Hear the Word of God: To do this, you must attend a church where Bible fundamentals are preached regularly, especially the plan of salvation made possible through the shed blood of Jesus Christ on the cross. You can also find sermons online or on livestream. The preached Word will help your faith to grow. When you watch the Seminoles play on TV, you listen to commentators. The same goes for attending church. Don't just make it a routine. Focus on what is happening and listen to the Word of God presented to you by a minister called by God.

Spurrier made changes because he wanted the Gators to win. Bowden, who was a great coach, kept the same game plan. As a Christian, you cannot keep a routine that does not grow your faith. So get out of your comfort zone, make the changes, and enjoy your life as a follower of Jesus Christ.

DAY 7

BE CAREFUL OF THE PRIDE INSIDE

January 1, 2013: Florida State 31, Northern Illinois 10
By Andy Clapp

The king exclaimed, 'Is this not Babylon the Great that I have built by my vast power to be a royal residence and to display my majestic glory?' —Daniel 4:30 HCSB

Be careful what you say. Confidence and arrogance can be easily misinterpreted based on the hearer.

Northern Illinois shook the college football world with a meteoric rise to the top fifteen in the nation. Jordan Lynch, their talented quarterback, terrorized their opponents with his arm and his legs. Yet, his mouth is what made news prior to the Orange Bowl and caught the attention of the Seminoles.

Ahead of the game, Lynch said FSU had never seen anything like the Huskies' offense. His prediction that they'd have the 'Noles "on their knees" by the fourth quarter sealed his fate in Florida.

With the game scoreless in the first quarter, Lynch kept the ball on third and four, trying to secure the Huskies' initial first down on their second possession. For a split second, Lynch appeared certain to make the 4 yards needed. But Kelvin Smith burst onto the scene and nearly decapitated the Northern Illinois Heisman candidate. The crowd erupted at the force of the tackle.

Within three minutes of the hit, the 'Noles struck on offense. Lonnie Pryor torched the Huskies' defense for a 60-yard touchdown.

That led to the 'Noles dominating the game and rocking Lynch like he's never been throttled before. Three sacks left a mark. Lynch threw a costly interception, and for the game, he completed less than 40 percent of his passes.

His coach said his quarterback spoke with confidence in the lead-up to the game. But instead, the Seminoles heard arrogance and were determined to humble the quarterback.

And at the end of the Orange Bowl, humbleness came from humiliation.

Pride comes before destruction, and an arrogant spirit before a fall. —Proverbs 16:18 HCSB

FEAR THE SPEAR

Confidence and arrogance aren't separated by too much. One slides from confidence into arrogance easily and often. Though confidence can be a strength, overconfidence and arrogance promise troubles will arise. Where is arrogance most often revealed? The words we speak give others an insight into our thoughts about ourselves. We identify arrogance easily in the lives of others but find it harder to see it in ourselves. What do your words sound like to those who hear them? Can you see areas of your life where arrogance may be developing and needs to be addressed? Either we grow in our humility, or we will be humbled in a more powerful manner.

'NOLE NATION

What arrogance promises is that humbling will occur—and the prideful inch closer to humiliation with every word spoken.

King Nebuchadnezzar learned the truth the hard way. As he stepped out one day, he absorbed the magnitude of Babylon and gave himself the credit for its greatness. He boasted about what he had done. He never imagined what the Lord would do as a result.

The Bible says that before Nebuchadnezzar finished the boastful statement of his greatness, the Lord banished him. The king took the place of the cattle. The one who fed on the choicest food before his exile now grazed on the field. Even his appearance altered after the humbling. He looked like royalty before; he resembled wildlife after the Lord tossed him out of the palace.

So many dangers arise when arrogance takes root in our lives. The Bible warns that it is pride that precedes a fall. Pride places priority on us, neglecting to acknowledge God's power and position. Arrogance infects a heart, causing the heart to believe that it has little to no need for God. Amazingly, the Lord humbles us for our own good when arrogance runs rampant in our lives.

The humbling of the Lord is often painful, just as it is purposeful. So, how can we identify arrogance in our lives to repent now and avoid a humbling later? Here are a few ideas:

1. Listen to yourself—take a moment to truly listen to what you say to those around you. Dissect how you speak and honestly assess your words.

2. Think about your mindset—have you elevated yourself above others? If we begin to think of ourselves as superior to others, our thoughts will eventually affect our words and actions. We wait to be served rather than looking for avenues to serve. Get the mindset right, and the trajectory of life will also be realigned.

3. Highlight the strengths of others rather than your own strength—a great way to avoid arrogance and pride is to point out what others are doing well in their lives. Making such a decision—a conscious effort—breeds humility in our lives.

4. Identify arrogance areas—see where pride could creep in and pray over those specific areas in life.

5. Acknowledge God and give Him the glory—without the Lord, we can do nothing. Acknowledge God's presence and provision in every area of life, and it will safeguard your life from arrogance.

The Huskies' quarterback set a bull's-eye on himself before the Orange Bowl, and the 'Noles made sure they hit the target. All that Lynch said before highlighted Florida State's dominance, pouring salt into the wound of a devastating defeat.

DAY 8
ROLE MODELS AT ALL TIMES

January 1, 1996: Florida State 31, Notre Dame 26
By Bethany Jett

> Show yourself in all respects to be a model of good
> works, and in your teaching show integrity, dignity,
> and sound speech that cannot be condemned, so that
> an opponent may be put to shame, having nothing evil
> to say about us. —Titus 2:7–8

The warm sun beat down on the crowd gathered to celebrate
the Orange Bowl, the biggest sporting event of my life up
until that point. My dad and I woke up early and drove to
Miami Gardens. Souvenirs and T-shirts and food stands lined
the pathway toward the stadium. Smells filled my nostrils, the
cool air filled my expanding lungs, and the giggles of coeds and
shouts of scalpers met my ears.

I started the game off as a Fighting Irish fan because I'm Irish,
and I was rooting for the "church school" along with my dad.

And then, after one of many great Florida State plays, I saw
a blonde girl in a garnet-and-gold jersey stand up a few rows
ahead of me and cheer with her friends.

And that was it.

In that moment, she was everything I wanted to be: free-spir-
ited, fun, independent, and rooting for a team she loved.

33

Perhaps it was my first act of teenage rebellion, but I gleefully began rooting for Florida State, a sudden shift with no warning, which made the game more fun to have my dad and me on competing sides.

And *we* won.

The Florida State Seminoles took the victory, and in my heart of hearts, I knew this was a love affair that would last a lifetime.

> Let no one despise you for your youth, but set the believers an example in speech, in conduct, in love, in faith, in purity. —1 Timothy 4:12

FEAR THE SPEAR

You never know who you are going to influence. The Bible says we need to conduct ourselves in a manner worthy of the Lord. Just like that young woman exemplified everything my fourteen-year-old self wanted to be, that pales in comparison to how we can point others to Christ by our actions.

People are always watching to see how Christians react, and aren't they quick to point out when someone is being hypocritical? It's a sad state of affairs, but we always represent Christ, even when we lose our temper or make a mistake.

More often than not, it's how we respond in bad situations that really give us a chance to show the difference that having a relationship with Jesus makes.

'NOLE NATION

The Bible says to be prepared in season and out of season. So, here are five ways we can be a good representation of Jesus.

Role Models at All Times

1. Demonstrate integrity. Do the right thing even when (*we think*) no one is looking . . . because someone usually is. Even more important, *God* is always watching.

2. Admit mistakes quickly. When we do something wrong, the best thing to do is acknowledge our role in the problem. This builds trust with our family, friends, and even in the business world.

3. Make restitution. The best question we can ask when we've messed up is, "How can I make the situation right?" This simple behavior sets us apart from those who leave others to clean up their messes.

4. Use edifying speech. Our *yes* should be *yes*, and our *no* should be *no*. Additionally, let's keep our talk wholesome and steer clear of cursing. When we can make our point without resorting to vulgarities, we demonstrate maturity and the ability to hold our tongues.

5. Go the extra mile. Can we stay a few extra minutes after an event and help clean up? Are there any needs that we can anticipate? Acts of service are small ways to show Christ's love, and their impact is always greatly felt.

Five seconds was all it took for my life to be forever changed by a college student at a football game. How much more can we change someone's life for eternity?

DAY 9
IT'S OK TO DEFEND YOURSELF

November 30, 1996: Florida State 24, Florida 21
By Del Duduit

For he is the minister of God to thee for good. But
if thou do that which is evil, be afraid; for he beareth
not the sword in vain: for he is the minister of God, a
revenger to execute wrath upon him that doeth evil.
—Romans 13:4 KJV

In a preview of the Sugar Bowl a few weeks away, Florida State
used a pounding defense to send a message to their future
opponents that they were for real.

The Seminoles swarmed and got to Florida quarterback
Danny Wuerffel at will.

He was chased, sacked seven times, and knocked down 25
times as FSU defeated the Gators, 24-21, at Doak Campbell
Stadium in Tallahassee in front of nearly 81,000 fans.

That was Florida State Head Coach Bobby Bowden's plan
all along. He wanted to show the college football world that his
defense was the best in the land.

The nation's No.-1 defense limited Wuerffel to 362 yards on
23 of 48 attempts and three touchdowns. But, more important,
the Gator QB was picked off three times.

On the other side of the ball, the FSU offense was led by
Warrick Dunn, who blazed away on the field for 185 yards

rushing. Florida Head Coach Steve Spurrier described Dunn as "sensational" and the "reason they won the game."

Seminole signal-caller Thad Busby finished the game with 124 yards passing and completed only 12 of 32 pass attempts.

But it was the defense that brought home the win.

In the second half, the Gators started to play from the shotgun formation, which Spurrier did not like to use. However, they were desperate and could not figure out how to maneuver around blockers to protect Wuerffel.

When the Gators had five blockers, the Seminoles sent six rushers. Each play, the 'Noles outmanned Florida and frustrated Spurrier's offensive game plan. Florida State confused the Gators to the point they could not get off a pass without their quarterback being sent to the turf.

In the end, the 'Noles came out on top with the 24-21 win and assured themselves of a spot in the national championship game.

> They which builded on the wall, and they that bare burdens, with those that laded, every one with one of his hands wrought in the work, and with the other hand held a weapon. For the builders, everyone had his sword girded by his side, and so builded. And he that sounded the trumpet was by me. —Nehemiah 4:17–18 KJV

Are there times when you feel you cannot score in life because you keep getting tackled by Satan's offense? How do followers of the Lord Jesus Christ defend themselves when threatened? Some might believe that Christians are supposed to turn the other cheek, but God expects us to stand up for ourselves and our beliefs.

FEAR THE SPEAR

As a child of God, you may be faced with a situation where you are in danger, but you don't take action to protect yourself. Others may try to take advantage of you because of your convictions, and they don't expect you to respond. Some think that followers of Christ should wilt and allow others to just walk all over them.

'NOLE NATION

Keep in mind that there are those who cannot defend themselves. God instructs us to defend those who cannot defend themselves. You cannot turn a blind eye to the evil that is going on around you. God expects you to stand up for what's right, and you will give an account on Judgment Day. So, what can you do to show true courage in the face of evil and protect the oppressed?

1. Show respect for the law: Pray for your first responders, police officers, and firefighters. When you see them, thank them in person for what they do to protect you and keep your community safe. When you honor those who serve you and put their lives on the line every day, you honor the Lord. God has placed these people in your life for your protection. Respect them and help them when needed. This can be done through prayer, public support, and financial donations. If you see a group of police at breakfast, buy them a round of coffee and tell them how much you appreciate their service. "Honour all men. Love the brotherhood. Fear God. Honour the king" (1 Peter 2: 17 KJV).

2. Be aware of your surroundings: Take action to protect your property. It's not as expensive as it used to be to install cameras and sensors around your home to alert you to intruders. If God has blessed you with resources, then consider taking action to keep your belongings safe.

3. Support a cause: If you are troubled about any issues, then get involved and make a difference. Allow God to bless you and speak up for those who cannot speak for themselves.

4. Know your rights: If your state allows you to legally carry a concealed firearm, then consider doing so. But follow all laws and be proactive. Educate yourself and pray for the Lord's guidance.

5. Be on guard: Over the past few years, there have been several church shootings that could have been avoided. Consider talking to your church leaders about forming a trained security team to help protect those who worship with you. Also, consult your local law enforcement department for guidance. "But if any provide not for his own, and specially for those of his own house, he hath denied the faith, and is worse than an infidel" (1 Timothy 5: 8 KJV).

Criminals do not have the right to take advantage of you because you are a kind and gentle person who loves Jesus. There is a time and place to be righteous. You can also pray a hedge of protection around you and your loved ones. God does not want you to become a vigilante, but you have the right to defend yourself and your property.

DAY 10
EVEN IN BAD TIMES, PRAISE THE LORD

November 13, 1993: FSU 24, Notre Dame 31
By Bethany Jett

I will bless the LORD at all times; his praise shall continually be in my mouth. —Psalm 34:1 ESV

No. 1-ranked Florida State came out swinging at Notre Dame Stadium in a matchup against the Number-2 ranked Fighting Irish. Both teams boasted a 9-0 record, which led ESPN to broadcast the game live from the stadium, the first time ever on a college campus: College Game Day broadcast.

Coming off the national championship, the Seminoles prepared to crush Notre Dame with their stellar offense, but the Fighting Irish's pass rush cemented this game into NCAA football history. Safety Shawn Wooden broke up a desperation pass on the final play to hand the 'Noles a defeat and shattered their dreams of a national championship.

The Florida State team had run over their opponents offensively in every game that season, but their defense was not as strong as it should have been, which allowed Notre Dame to sweep in with an offense that the FSU defense was not prepared for.

Despite all that Florida State had going for them, Notre Dame kicked their garnet-and-gold booties that day in South Bend.

The game ended with a sobering loss for the Seminoles at 24 points to the Fighting Irish's 31.

But they who wait for the Lord shall renew their strength; they shall mount up with wings like eagles; they shall run and not be weary; they shall walk and not faint. —Isaiah 40:31 ESV

FEAR THE SPEAR

Despite their devastating loss to Notre Dame, Florida State went on to win the national championship and Charlie Ward took home the Heisman, but the road to the Promised Land wasn't without a little pain on the way.

When God led the Israelites out of Egypt, how could they imagine they would end up wandering the desert for forty years? Where was the land overflowing with milk and honey? Their leaders were strong. Moses was in constant communion with God, and Joshua was the favorite to lead the people to God's victory.

Obviously, a football game cannot compare to what the Israelites went through. Still, the comparison of the world watching, expecting greatness, only to witness a turn of events that no one saw coming is similar.

How often do we find ourselves in situations where we knew we were following God's planning, when we were on top of the world—where everything we touched turned to proverbial gold—only to see it fall away temporarily before the blessing came?

The Israelites were led out of Egypt by God. They witnessed His presence in the pillar of light. They saw Him through the glow on Moses's face. But then the victory was out of reach. A new generation had to come into place before God allowed the passage of His promise to come to pass.

'NOLE NATION

We praise God when He provides for us, but when circumstances get tight, we wonder where He is. So here are five ways we can remember His goodness, no matter what we're going through.

1. Reflect. Make a list of the times that God has shown up in your life. Then, when you're struggling, you'll have a record of God's faithfulness.

2. Record. Write down your current prayer requests and praises in a notebook. Use index cards and highlight the requests after they are answered.

3. Ask for wisdom and discernment. Is there a situation or sin issue in your life that you need to change?

4. Move. What can you do to move the needle for your current situation? If tasks feel overwhelming, start by making a list of the big, overall categories. Then start writing down what needs to happen to complete each task. Here is a simple example: Clean the Kitchen. Under that heading, you could write: 1. Unload and load dishwasher. 2. Wash pans. 3. Put away food and take

out the trash. 4. Wipe down counters. Even if you don't get all those smaller jobs done at once, you can move the needle by taking the steps one at a time.

5. Wait. Sometimes God isn't waiting on you. He's waiting on something (or someone) else. Patience is difficult when we feel like we're up against a wall.

The Israelites were not perfect. They celebrated their salvation from slavery by worshipping a golden calf, for heaven's sake. We may wonder how they could be so forgetful of what God has done, but we'd do better to not demonstrate that same behavior!

DAY 11
LEAVE NO ROOM FOR DOUBT

October 9, 1993: Florida State 28, Miami 10
By Andy Clapp

Enter through the narrow gate. For the gate is wide and
the road is broad that leads to destruction, and there
are many who go through it. —Matthew 7:13 HCSB

The Seminoles' nemesis entered Doak Campbell Stadium. In
years past, close losses to the Miami Hurricanes had derailed the
national championship plans for the 'Noles. A failed two-point
conversion left Florida State with a one-point loss in 1987. In
that game, FSU led 19-3 in the third quarter but fell short at the
end. Wide Right I and Wide Right II kept the Seminoles out of
the national championship in 1991 and 1992. If the men from
Tallahassee wanted to take the next step as a program, they
needed to beat Miami. The best way was to keep it from being
close at the end.

Sean Jackson shredded the 'Canes' defense on FSU's third
play from scrimmage. Jackson cut to the right, and 69 yards
later, the Seminoles led, 7-0.

Miami tied the game later in the first quarter, but Charlie
Ward hit Matt Frier for a seventy-two-yard touchdown pass,
and Ward scored on a keeper to put the home team up 21-7 at
the half.

In the fourth quarter, the game remained too close for comfort. The 'Noles' defense held strong, but the lead of 21-10 felt too tight.

It was the defense, however, that put the game away.

Miami had possession, trying to drive the ball down the field and pull closer. With any score, the game would be a one-score game, giving the 'Canes a chance to spoil the Seminoles' season again.

But Devin Bush put any doubts to rest. He intercepted Costa's pass and took the ball 40 yards for a touchdown.

FSU left no room for doubt, continuing their march toward a championship. They learned from previous seasons and dominated the Hurricanes.

> Then He said to them all, "If anyone wants to come with Me, he must deny himself, take up his cross daily, and follow Me." —Luke 9:23 HCSB

FEAR THE SPEAR

There is a temptation in life to push the limits and even live a bit dangerously. Though it's more rampant in our younger days, there can be a draw to being too cavalier in some areas of life even as we age. In what areas of life do you do the basic essentials just to get by? Where in your life do you take chances that can cost you later on? There is a belief that we can ride the fence in life and faith, a dangerous temptation that has overcome many. The Spirit tells us to go all-in with Jesus while the flesh tells us to live it up on earth.

'NOLE NATION

Jesus called everyone to make a choice. As He spoke to a multitude gathered on a hillside, He laid out a blueprint for life, one glorifying the Father. And as He neared the end of the Sermon on the Mount, He implored that they choose the narrow gate, to take the road to righteousness and leave no doubt about the outcome of life.

He gave examples. He said that some would stand before Him one day, professing what their good works were, only to be told to depart from Him. He later explained that following Him meant one had to take up a cross daily and follow Him. His words revealed His heart for us to ensure we are with Him in life.

Paul later instructed the Thessalonian believers to be sure and insulate their lives. Rather than dabble in the world, instead of playing with that which could pull them away, Paul commanded they stay as far away from evil as possible. He wrote, "Stay away from every kind of evil" (1 Thessalonians 5:22 HCSB). Rather than flirt with danger that can overtake you, keep as far away from it as possible.

Leave no room for doubt in your life or your testimony. Take the approach that ensures that you are a child of God, an approach that leaves others with an absolute assurance of where you stand in your life. How can we improve in that area of life? Here are some things to think about:

1. Choose Jesus—the only way to the Father is only through the Son. Jesus proclaimed that truth in John 14:6, and that choice alone leaves no doubt as to where you will spend eternity. Choose Jesus today and push forward in Christ starting this minute.

2. Seek Righteousness—by firmly seeking what is right, we put a distance between ourselves and the enemy's camp. That doesn't mean the enemy won't try to cause us to fall, but it will help us identify his tactics more easily.

3. Live the Word—Jesus followed the teaching of the narrow gate with another about firm foundations in life. He said to build your life on the rock by not only hearing His words but by acting on them.

4. Identify evil and push it out—if it's not of God, it's not going to lead you to victory in life. See what destroys and throw it out of your life.

5. Slam the door—Refuse to let the enemy back in. When the Lord helps you rid your life of something destructive, don't give an inch for it to return.

FSU needed to overcome Miami to realize its ultimate dream at the end of the season. Miami loomed ahead on the schedule, and the 'Canes had to be dealt with. The 'Noles were close before, but in 1993, they left no room for doubt. They were done with Miami and left no opening for chaos to spoil their dreams.

DAY 12
JUST HOLD ON

December 3, 2005: Florida State 27, Virginia Tech 22
By Del Duduit

Let not your hearts be troubled. Believe in God; believe
also in me. —John 14:1 ESV

By the end of the third quarter in the 2005 Dr Pepper ACC
Championship Game, the Florida State Seminoles held an
insurmountable 27-3 lead. The inaugural conference championship game was all but won.

But the No. 5-ranked Hokies of Virginia Tech had one final
quarter to make a comeback. And they made the most of it
at Alltel Stadium in Jacksonville, Florida. Head Coach Frank
Beamer mounted a surge that shook FSU Coach Bobby Bowden
and his No.-22 ranked 'Noles to the core.

Down by 24 points, quarterback Marcus Vick found Josh
Morgan for a 28-yard TD strike with 13:03 to play in regula-
tion. The Hokies went for the two-point conversation but failed
and trailed 27-9.

The Seminoles were forced to punt after a three-and-out
and gave the ball back to Virginia Tech.

A pass interference call on the 'Noles gave the Hokies a
first down. On the next play, Vick connected with Morgan for
a 50-yard gain to the FSU nine.

Two plays later, Vick scrambled 4 yards for a TD and cut the score to 27-15 with 10:50 to play.

Florida State only needed to put together a drive to run the clock down but couldn't make the first down and had to punt again.

The Hokies took over at their own 30 with plenty of time on the clock. But this time, Bowden's defense stiffened and sacked Vick, forcing Tech to punt as well.

When FSU got the ball back, the Hokies used two of their timeouts, and the 'Noles punted again.

Virginia Tech moved the ball downfield. Vick found Morgan for a 14-yard gain and followed with a 10-yarder to Cedric Humes. Next, a 19-yard gain from Vick to Jeff King moved the ball into Seminole territory. Then a roughing-the-passer call on FSU brought Virginia Tech another 15 yards closer to the end zone. Two plays later, Vick ran into the end zone from 2 yards out for the score with 1:44 to play.

Nineteen unanswered points by Virginia Tech.

An onside kick was the expected call because the Hokies were out of timeouts and needed the ball back, and Bowden placed his sure ball handlers upfront in expectation.

But somehow, Virginia Tech's Xavier Adibi seemed to have recovered the kick. But he had pounced on the ball before it traveled 10 yards, which is not allowed by rules.

Florida State was awarded the ball and ran out the clock to hold on for the win.

What a comeback from Virginia Tech! But FSU had weathered the storm and claimed the crown.

What will you do when Satan's team tries an onside kick? Will you finish well?

Who gave himself for our sins to deliver us from the present evil age, according to the will of our God and Father. —Galatians 1:4 ESV

FEAR THE SPEAR

Have you ever found yourself in a stressful situation? Maybe you are coming down to the wire, and you need to hear from God. Perhaps you want the Lord to show up and save the day, but you have not heard from Him. Maybe the stresses of a situation are mounting, and you need assurance from the Master that everything will be all right. Have your trust and faith ever been tried to the point where you doubted God's power? Have you ever felt like just throwing in the towel?

'NOLE NATION

The pressures of life can come to a boil and attack your faith. This is exactly what the forces of evil desire. They want you to doubt. They want you to give up. But this is the time your faith must take a stand. When the enemy makes a fourth-quarter run, puts points on the board, and you *must* recover the onside kick. Here are some ways to trust God, even when your circumstances seem hopeless.

1. Check out God's credentials: He is called the Master of the Sea for a reason. He raised the dead and healed the sick. He even provides for the sparrows. He shut the lions' mouths for Daniel, and He walked around in the fire with Shadrach, Meshach, and Abednego. He's got this. He knows what He's doing. And He will never let you down. "Your faithfulness continues through all

generations; you established the earth, and it endures" (Psalm 119:90 NIV).

2. Get ready and hold on: Coach Bowden held on and waited for the time to expire. Sometimes God asks us to wait on His timing before he calms the storm. Nothing happens to us without God's approval, and you must trust that He has the perfect plan for your life and your future.

3. Let go of what you cannot control. Don't ask God to take your problems away, but instead, give your problems to Him. Don't hold on to your worries. Give them to God and enjoy the freedom He has for you. "When I am afraid, I put my trust in you. In God, whose word I praise, in God I trust; I shall not be afraid. What can flesh do to me?" (Psalm 56:3–4 ESV).

4. Thank Him: Give Him gratitude before He answers your prayers and afterward. Praise Him for the prayers He did not answer because He had something better for you. He supplies all your needs. Keep a journal of everything Christ has done for you. If you can praise Him in the tough times, the good times will be even better. "I give thanks to my God always for you because of the grace of God that was given you in Christ Jesus" (1 Corinthians 1:4 ESV).

When the devil makes a run at you to try to win the game, remember that God still has another play to call. Spoiler alert—read the last chapter in the Bible. We already know that God wins in the end, and Satan will be punished for all eternity. "And the great dragon was thrown down, that ancient serpent, who is called the devil and Satan, the deceiver of the whole world—he was thrown down to the earth, and his angels were thrown down with him" (Revelation 12:9 ESV).

YOU WIN!

DAY 13
THERE'S TIME FOR A COMEBACK

November 26, 1994: Florida State 31, Florida 31
By Andy Clapp

Therefore we do not give up. Even though our outer
person is being destroyed, our inner person is being
renewed day by day. —2 Corinthians 4:16 HCSB

A rivalry game turned into a rout. The Gators invaded Doak
Campbell Stadium in 1994, and when time ran out in the
third quarter, the men from Gainesville held a 31-3 lead. The
defending national champion Seminoles stood on the cusp of a
home blowout to one of their most hated rivals.

Florida State struck first as Dan Mowery connected on a
first-quarter field goal. From there, the Gators owned the next
thirty minutes of the game.

Danny Wuerffel torched the Seminole defense, throwing three
touchdowns in the first half. After that, Florida's 24 unanswered
points gave them a commanding 24-3 lead. Then, in the third
quarter, Wuerffel found the end zone again, this time running the
ball in, leading the Gators to believe the game was put away.

But when the fourth quarter began, the Seminoles awoke.

Zack Crockett bulled his way into the end zone for the
first 'Noles touchdown. Then, when Florida's offense, which
had been humming all day, failed to get a first down, the door
opened a little further for a comeback.

Less than a minute later, Danny Kanell hit Andre Cooper for a touchdown.

The defense again smothered Florida's offense.

Bobby Bowden's team went no-huddle, trying to tighten the game even more. Kanell scampered in for the third touchdown of the quarter, drawing FSU to within seven.

Wuerffel began a march with the Gators, but James Colzie picked off an errant pass, giving the 'Noles a final chance. With less than two minutes left, Rock Preston scored and tied the game.

The Choke at the Doak lives on in the minds of both teams. The drive of the 'Noles pushed them to keep chipping away, even when the deficit seemed insurmountable.

But as for you, be strong; don't be discouraged, for your work has a reward. —2 Chronicles 15:7 HCSB

FEAR THE SPEAR

Do the odds seem to be stacked against you today? Life presents times where the most logical decision is to give up and go on with life. Others chime in with their thoughts about the inevitable defeat, increasing the weight of the situation. As most of the world cuts its losses and gives up, we feel the temptation to do the same. Why does it matter if we quit? Does it really impact anyone if we mail it in when we face insurmountable odds? The debt is too great to overcome. You're too far behind to salvage your job. The relationship derailed long ago. What if there was still time for a comeback? What if the insurmountable became something you could overcome?

'NOLE NATION

The apostle Paul had a list of reasons to give up. From the beginning days of his conversion and ministry, opposition mounted. So dire was the threat at the earliest stages of his ministry that Paul had to be snuck outside the city under the cloak of night to avoid execution.

Paul, even with the odds stacked against the gospel movement, refused to give in or give up. His attitude encourages us even today. Paul wrote of the pressure but pointed to the passion. He told the Corinthians that they may be destroyed outwardly, but inwardly, they were being renewed. The enemy threw all he had at Paul and his team, but they continued pressing on for the kingdom.

Giving up is never a mark of a committed Christian. Though the task or the obstacles standing in the way may appear impossible to overcome, we know that nothing is impossible for God. His abilities are far greater than anything we face.

Throughout time, God has proved His power to overcome even the greatest odds stacked against His purpose. When three Hebrews faced a fiery furnace, He walked in the fire with them. When the children of Israel had no way out, He parted the sea, providing the way out. When evil landed what seemed to be a final blow on Friday, Sunday came, and Jesus emerged as the victor.

So, how do we keep going when we face the impossible? Here are a few suggestions:

1. Take one step—every step toward fixing a problem or overcoming a deficit brings us a step closer to victory. A mountain isn't climbed in a single leap. That first step begins the ascent to the top.

2. Change your focus—use scripture to remind yourself of God's ability. See it as His battle. Speak and stand on the truth of the Bible as it will help overcome discouragement along the way.

3. Determine to press forward—those who allow the idea of quitting to fester in their minds are vulnerable to choosing that as an option. Refuse to allow quitting to creep into your mind. Determine that you will do what you can do.

4. Assess the long-term effects of quitting—those who easily quit set a standard for themselves. If you quit once, quitting becomes an option always. See the urge to quit as dangerously detrimental, not only today, but years from now. One of the worst long-term effects of giving up is the constant wondering of what might have been if we pressed on a little longer.

5. Find what inspires you to keep going—find some music, a few Bible verses, or even a person who overcame similar struggles and use that to pick you up when times are hard.

The Gators believed they had the victory, but the 'Noles made the necessary plays, refusing to accept defeat. The comeback still marks conversations today. The 'Noles showed their heart and did what most thought impossible.

DAY 14
THE DAY OF REDEMPTION

September 5, 2005: FSU 10, Miami 7
By Bethany Jett

Who shall separate us from the love of Christ? Shall
tribulation, or distress, or persecution, or famine, or
nakedness, or danger, or sword? . . . No, in all these
things we are more than conquerors through him who
loved us. —Romans 8:35, 37 ESV

When Florida State and the University of Miami play, you're
guaranteed that fans are waiting for the inevitable Wide Right
comments. With wide rights in 1991, 1992, 2000, 2003, and
2004, and one wide left in 2002, FSU and Miami matchups are
famous for their missed kicks.

The Seminoles-Hurricanes rivalry is rooted in pride by
FSU, one of the few teams that ensures the Miami team is on
their roster every year. Bobby Bowden joked that written on
his tombstone would be the words, "At least he played Miami."

The 2005 matchup brought some vindication to the
Seminoles, even though with a score of 10-7, this is a game that
does not go down in the history books of high scores.

Forget Wide Right or Wide Left—with 2:16 left in the
game, Miami lined up for a 28-yard field goal, but Jon Peattie
didn't even get a chance to kick the ball because the holder
Brian Monroe dropped the snap and the ball bounced away.

Redemption.

"We finally stole one from them like they've been stealing them from us," Florida State Head Coach Bobby Bowden said. "It's about time."[2]

Both quarterbacks—FSU's Drew Weatherford and Miami's Kyle Wright—were first-time starters, and their offenses struggled from the get-go. The inability of both teams to complete passes in the second half resulted in the game ending with a 10-7 final score.

Even though the game was full of rough plays, including the Miami Muff, sports podcaster Nate Donley comments, "All that matters is the final score. The torment of losing to Miami for six straight games was finally over."

Indeed. Despite the difficulties, this fiftieth matchup between FSU and UM ended Florida State's six-game losing streak against the Hurricanes since the 1999 Wire-to-Wire season.

And considering Miami has "played more games against FSU than any other team," FSU is always ready for another matchup, with hopefully no more Wide Rights to add to the list.

In him we have redemption through his blood, the forgiveness of our trespasses, according to the riches of his grace. —Ephesians 1:7 ESV

FEAR THE SPEAR

What's impressive about FSU's continued matchup with Miami, even after six straight losses, is that they poured their

---

[2] "Late Hurricanes Mistake Seals Win for Seminoles," ESPN.com, September 6, 2005, https://www.espn.com/college-football/recap/_/gameId/252480052.

heart and soul into the game, knowing that failure was a possibility . . . again.

There are times in our lives when we work hard, do our best, and still end up on the losing side. But a sign of maturity is persevering through hardship.

Failure is where mistakes are made, and experience is born. Through the struggle and adversity, we learn to dial in on what is most important, and many times, we are humbled, falling to our knees before the throne of God.

Hardship is part of this world, but through God's might, He allows for a change in circumstances, and we finally get the momentum we need to push ahead and overcome. And oh . . . what a beautiful feeling it is knowing that we've been redeemed.

'NOLE NATION

Say what you like about Florida State, but unlike the jorts-filled orange-and-blue school, FSU will play the Hurricanes, even during the years they know it's just gonna hurt their win-loss record. We grow through our struggles, and playing the tough teams in life helps us grow. Here are five things we can learn from hardship:

1. We learn our limitations. It's OK to stretch our boundaries and find out just how much we can do. Too many people never realize the magnitude of what they are capable of simply because they give up when the situation gets difficult. Knowing where our limits are allows us to make clear-headed decisions in the future.

2. We see where we can grow. If we don't stretch ourselves, we won't be able to push ourselves in areas where we could really flourish.

3. We can keep similar situations from happening again . . . and maybe keep others from walking down a similar path. Learning from other people's mistakes is a sign of wisdom. We can be great mentors and role models for others by sharing our own mishaps and helping others to avoid making the same mistake.

4. We have the chance to practice humility and, in some cases, reconciliation.

5. When others are involved, we get insight into their personalities and can make future decisions based on how they reacted when the chips were down.

Losing is never fun. Making mistakes with the world watching is absolutely embarrassing. But it is through the hardship, the purifying process, that we are refined.

DAY 15
WE ARE NEW CREATIONS

FSU Culture: The Sod Cemetery
By Bethany Jett

Therefore, if anyone is in Christ, he is a new creation.
The old has passed away; behold, the new has come.
—2 Corinthians 5:17 ESV

When you tour the Florida State campus, be sure to pay your respects to the teams that have suffered at the hands of our Seminoles by visiting the infamous Sod Cemetery. The graveyard holds patches of grass from the fields of teams the 'Noles defeated, a tradition started in 1962 when Dean Coyle Moore, a professor and FSU athletic board member, challenged the team to "bring back some sod from the between the hedges at Georgia."

Florida State won that game against the Bulldogs in a shutout match: 18-0. The sod was presented to Moore in a paper Coca-Cola cup. The sod was buried on the practice field, and a sign with the date, score, and name of the opposing team marked the spot.

With that, a tradition was born.

There are three criteria for sod to be buried in the cemetery:

1.   Games on the road where FSU is the underdog.

2.   All road games at the University of Florida.

3.   All ACC championship and bowl games.

If a win happens at one of these games, the captains bring back a piece of the opposing team's field, which is then buried under a plaque bearing the team's namesake. And for the teams that play at Florida State—special flowers in their teams' colors adorn the gravesites of the sod taken from years prior—a memorandum of the beatdown that took place in years past.

As of this writing, 107 patches of opposing teams' sod are growing in the Tallahassee dirt across from the practice field in a special greenspace, waiting for the next FSU win.

FEAR THE SPEAR

The Sod Cemetery is full of death that regained new life, and oh, there are so many verses that apply.

"He has made everything beautiful in its time." (Ecclesiastes 3:11 ESV)

"And I will give you a new heart, and a new spirit I will put within you." (Ezekiel 36:26 ESV)

And perhaps my favorite verse (admittedly taken a little out of context) comes from Isaiah 65:17, "For behold, I create new heavens and a new earth, and *the former things shall not be remembered*" (emphasis mine). The "former things" being the losing team . . . which, of course, FSU ensures is memorialized with the grave marker.

But all kidding aside, the concept of death coming to life is integral to the Christian faith. The sod dies once it's pulled from the field. Our souls are dead with sin.

But the roots are restored once they're planted in the cemetery, and new life comes forth as it mixes with the life already there.

Once we are saved and are planted deep with Christ.

We are new creations in Christ. Our old lives are gone, and we take comfort that our Savior is in heaven creating a new home for us.

> And if I go and prepare a place for you, I will come again and will take you to myself, that where I am you may be also. —John 14:3 ESV

'NOLE NATION

Are there any areas in your life that need tending? Here are five requests for us to ask God so He can cultivate a new heart in us:

1. Ask God to search your heart and show you the areas that you need to work on. This is not for the faint of heart, for having God open our eyes to the dark spots in our life can be difficult to admit.

2. Ask God to help us seek Him. 1 Kings 8:58 says, "that he may incline our hearts to Him, to walk in all His ways, and to keep His commandments" (ESV).

3. Ask God for wisdom. King Solomon was able to ask God for literally anything, and in his wisdom, he asked for wisdom. That request was not only for Solomon. The Bible says, "If anyone lacks wisdom, let him ask God" (James 1:5 ESV). We should never think that we've "made it" when it comes to seeking wisdom because the Bible also says that if you "Give instruction to a wise man, he will be still wiser; teach a righteous man, and he will increase in learning" (Proverbs 9:9 ESV).

Del Duduit, Andy Clapp, and Bethany Jett

4. Ask God for strength. It's a lie straight from the devil that we can do anything within our own strength or power. 2 Chronicles tells us that God will "strengthen those whose hearts are fully committed to him" (2 Chronicles 16:9 NIV). Ask God for strength and to use you to showcase His glory.

5. Ask God for patience. The sanctification process is not instantaneous, so we need to be able to go the distance.

Praise be to God for allowing us to cast off our former selves. We take heart because "We were buried therefore with him by baptism into death, in order that, just as Christ was raised from the dead by the glory of the Father, we too might walk in newness of life" (Romans 6:4 ESV).

DAY 16
PRESS ON, PUSHING THROUGH THE PAIN

October 10, 2015: Florida State 29, Miami 24
By Andy Clapp

A man who endures trials is blessed, because when he passes the test he will receive the crown of life that God has promised to those who love Him. —James 1:12 HCSB

Questions arose about Dalvin Cook's health. A hamstring injury for a running back raises red flags. Cook sat out of practice early in the week, but nothing prevented him from taking the field on Saturday night.

This was FSU-Miami.

This was the game of all games for the season.

Would he be 50 percent of his normal self or even 75 percent? The answer came in the first time he took a pitch from quarterback Everett Golson.

Four consecutive passes marked the plan to start the game, leading the 'Noles to their own 27. Golson ran wide to his left, an option play set up. Golson drew the defender, pitched to Cook at the last second, and the running back torched the 'Canes for a seventy-three-yard touchdown. The run gave Florida State a 7-0 lead, but the game was far from finished.

After Miami kicked a field goal, the 'Noles rushed down the field. Golson connected with his tight end for a long reception to get into Miami territory. A couple of plays later, Golson hit Cook on a short checkdown. He dashed toward the sideline and turned toward the end zone. The short pass, designed to pick up 5 to seven yards, went for more as Cook made the amazing cut inside the ten and scored again, pushing the lead to 14-3.

The Hurricanes fought back. While the 'Noles kicked three field goals, the 'Canes scored touchdowns. When Stacy Coley caught a twenty-nine-yard pass from Brad Kaaya, the 'Canes led 24-23 with ten minutes to go in the fourth quarter.

The Seminoles turned again to Dalvin Cook. Slipping a tackle and accelerating to the end zone, Cook scored on a 23-yard run, giving the 'Noles the victory. The hurting running back ran for 222 yards and scored three touchdowns. The game meant that much.

> For our momentary light affliction is producing for us
> an absolutely incomparable eternal weight of glory.
> —2 Corinthians 4:17 HCSB

FEAR THE SPEAR

Trials come in every area of life. Right now, you may face a physical trial that takes all you've got to get through a day. Financial trials threaten to ruin our lives. Today, you may not be at your very best, but there is an opportunity for victory. Over time, the wear and tear of life itself batters us mentally, emotionally, and spiritually. But the payoff of pushing through far outweighs the pain endured along the way. There is still much to be done. There will never be another today. This game only comes once.

'NOLE NATION

What comes from enduring the drudges of life and persevering through the pain? What can help you to push through in life?

The early church knew trials and tribulation. The ancient world tested the resiliency of the early believers on a daily basis. As James wrote his letter, he commented on the trials of life. Rather than bemoan the reality of the tests faced or question why God allowed such things to occur, James shifted the perspective. He saw the trials as less of a burden and more of a production line to a blessing.

James explained that those who endured the tests and trials were blessed because of what came as a result. He pointed out that endurance resulted from being pushed to the limits. Ultimately, he wrote that perseverance until the end resulted in an eternal reward. The effort had a prize, a crown, but only those willing to push through all that life threw at them received the reward.

Push through the pains of this day. Seize the opportunity before you because today will never come around again. You are playing for something bigger today and what you overcome to get to the goal gives even greater glory to the Lord at the end of the journey.

Don't give up only to look back and dream later of what might have been. Instead, put on the pads and bust through the line on a quest toward victory.

Here are a few tips for persevering that might help you suit up when you feel like you are not at one hundred percent:

1. Endurance building makes the next obstacle more manageable—what you overcome today will build up your resiliency for whatever may come next. Furthermore, when you overcome today's giant, you will see that you can handle even more later.

2. Focus on the end prize—the pain can be managed more when we focus on what can come if we push through. Focus on the outcome rather than only seeing the effort required to get there.

3. Praise the Lord even in the trial—you were given the opportunity. Praise the Lord that He chose you. Praise Him that He gives you what you need to overcome.

4. Remember the disciples who overcame massive obstacles—find inspiration in the disciples who faced challenges and persevered through, refusing to throw in the towel. Let their stories uplift you to push through so that your story might uplift someone else one day.

5. Give it all you've got—lay it all out on the field of your life. Give every ounce. Others will see the effort and you will not have to second-guess yourself later.

Dalvin Cook came through on the national stage. Though there were questions before the game about his availability, there were no questions at the end about his heart.

DAY: 17

CHANGING OF THE GUARD

September 3, 1994: Florida State 41, Virginia 17
By Andy Clapp

Timothy, my son, I am giving you this instruction in keeping with the prophecies previously made about you, so that by them you may strongly engage in battle, having faith and a good conscience. —1 Timothy 1:18–19 HCSB

A new year, a new quarterback—Danny Kanell—and a new offensive coordinator—Mark Richt—marked a showdown with the conference foe, the Virginia Cavaliers.

The offense struggled early. A Kanell interception set up Virginia for a field goal to take a 3-0 lead. For the first few series, the offense looked out of sync. The 'Noles' defense held strong while the offense worked out the bugs.

In the waning seconds of the first quarter, Danny Kanell hit Warrick Dunn on a swing pass. The two-yard pass became a 53-yard gain as Dunn used his speed and strength to break tackles and race down the sidelines. When the second quarter began, Dunn took another short pass and scored. Though Scott Bentley's extra-point attempt was blocked, momentum had swung in favor of the 'Noles.

With less than five minutes left in the second quarter, the new quarterback tossed his second touchdown of the game, hitting Billy Glenn to extend the lead.

Virginia fumbled inside their own twenty, and FSU recovered the miscue. Kanell hit Kez McCorvey for the next score. The offense clicked with two touchdowns in less than a minute. The 'Noles led 20-3, and the fans could breathe easier as Mark Richt's offense looked good.

In the third quarter, the ground game flexed its muscle. Rock Preston ran the ball in from 3 yards out to expand the lead to 27-3. Zack Crockett pounded the ball in from one yard out later in the quarter, essentially putting the game out of reach.

A fourth-quarter touchdown pass from Kanell to McCorvey finished the scoring, giving the Seminoles six touchdowns on the day and a victory to start a new season. Brad Scott had moved on to the SEC, but Bobby Bowden chose the right man to fill the post.

> Go, therefore, and make disciples of all nations, baptizing them in the name of the Father and of the Son and of the Holy Spirit, teaching them to observe everything I have commanded you. And remember, I am with you always, to the end of the age. —Matthew 28:19–20 HCSB

FEAR THE SPEAR

You have the opportunity to help others to reach their dreams. Around us stands talented people who need a shot to make things happen. What if the opportunity you give to them today changes the trajectory of your life and theirs and countless others? Have you taken stock of those around you to see what they have to offer in life? We are often put into places to help elevate others. Only those who know the strengths of those around them elevate the right people and keep pushing forward toward the goal.

'NOLE NATION

One of the greatest blessings in life is helping others achieve their dreams and fulfill God's calling in their lives. When we equip others, we show godly leadership. Mark Richt later said that Bobby Bowden not only furthered his career as a coach but also helped Richt grow in his walk with Christ. Bowden saw potential in Richt and worked to bring out that gift in the young man.

Paul worked likewise in the life of young Timothy. Paul mentioned the calling on Timothy's life, mentioning the prophesies spoken over the young pastor's life. Paul sought to equip God's chosen leader so he would thrive in ministry and stand strong when the enemy attacked. Paul longed to see his protégé be successful in his work and in his personal walk with Christ.

Similarly, Jesus put the disciples in place to go out and fulfill the calling on their lives. For three years, He taught them how to live. He equipped them through what they saw and all they heard. Then, as He prepared to ascend into heaven, He gave them the final call. The Great Commission came as a result of Jesus putting the pieces in place to advance the kingdom.

And the mission carried on. When we live out our lives, we have the chance to leave a good legacy or a bad one. A simple step toward a great legacy is helping others fulfill their purpose in life. Here are a few legacy building ideas:

1. See the strengths of others—We easily identify the weaknesses of those around us. Take the opportunity to build a relationship with those around you and recognize their strengths. Recognizing the strength of someone helps us to put them in the right position, not just any position.

2. Be less competitive—We live in a world filled with competition. See the success of others as a positive result rather than always trying to compete.

3. Encourage with words—Be the cheerleader of those around you. Champion their successes even more than you speak of your own. Our words can help others to reach new heights in their lives.

4. Look for opportunities for others to use their gifts—Match up the strength of those around you with opportunities around you. Help them get in a position to carry out their calling in life.

5. Help them succeed—Be a listening ear when needed. Give guidance to help them thrive. Serve them and help them when they need an extra set of hands and feet.

Bobby Bowden had a position to fill when Brad Scott left the 'Noles to coach South Carolina. Bowden had his choice of any coach, but he promoted Mark Richt and supported his offensive coordinator. Richt eventually took the job as the head coach of the Georgia Bulldogs, but he never forgot how Bobby Bowden helped him reach new heights.

DAY 18
LAUGHTER IS GOOD FOR THE SOUL

November 5, 1988: Florida State 59, South Carolina 0
By Del Duduit

Then our mouth was filled with laughter, and our
tongue with shouts of joy; then they said among the
nations, The LORD has done great things for them.
—Psalm 126:2 ESV

Not much to say about this game except the Seminoles
dominated the Gamecocks in every way. There was nothing
funny about the blowout at Williams-Brice Stadium for the
75,000 South Carolina fans.

The 'Noles forced a turnover on the Gamecocks' first
possession to give quarterback Peter Tom Willis and the offense
a crack at the scoreboard. Willis had the first start of his career
because Chip Ferguson was injured. Willis dropped back on the
team's second play from scrimmage, gave a pump fake to freeze
the linebackers, and let loose a pass that found Terry Anthony
for a 44-yard touchdown.

Later in the first quarter, South Carolina had to punt again.
But this time, FSU's Anthony Moss blocked the punt, recovered
the ball, and galloped into the end zone for a 14-0 lead.

The Gamecocks didn't know what hit them, especially
after Lawrence Dawsey caught two touchdown passes to boost
the score to 31-0 at the half. And things only got worse for

South Carolina in front of their home crowd, which obviously was not happy.

But leave it to the 'Noles' "Mr. Everything," Deion Sanders, who put a smile on the faces of the demoralized fans. During a timeout in the second half, Sanders stood up on the bench and faced the unhappy Gamecocks crowd. He started to yell at them and said, "Demand your money back. This is ridiculous. You need to leave now and demand a refund."

The crowd soon realized what he was saying and started to take note.

Then a teammate gave Sanders a megaphone so his message could be heard by even more fans. He implored the crowd to demand their money back—in a jovial way.

The fans chuckled, laughed, and took the humor as a sign to not take life so seriously. While they may have not liked their team's poor performance on the field, South Carolina fans left with smiles on their faces because Sanders's good-natured antics cheered them up.

He will yet fill your mouth with laughter, and your lips with shouting. —Job 8:21 ESV

Humor and laughter are essential parts of a healthy and Christian life.

FEAR THE SPEAR

Have you ever been in a situation where you wanted to giggle or smile when it was completely out of place? The more you try not to laugh, the harder it gets to keep a straight face. You are not alone. There is a time to mourn and a time to be cheerful, and you should never mix those moments up. But try not to take yourself so seriously that you never laugh or smile.

'NOLE NATION

Everyone faces troubles and crises in life. And while there are situations where it is totally inappropriate to crack up laughing, a lighthearted response can often diffuse a tense situation. We all have heartaches, but God can reduce the heavy load by using good friends to bring joy and laughter into your life. Here are some spiritual reasons why you *should* laugh and have fun more often.

1. It's healthy to laugh: According to some studies, your brain releases chemicals to reduce stress in your body when you laugh. It can help reduce your pain and put the kibosh on negative thoughts. Laughter can ease tension and help mourners through a grieving process.

2. It can drive away fear and doubt: Some folks might see humor as irreverent and childish. No one expects you to burst out in laughter during a sermon or a funeral service. It does not take the place of common sense. But it can provide comfort when you feel discouraged from the fight. Don't take yourself so seriously that you beat yourself up all the time and can't laugh at yourself when you make a mistake. Use your failures as a learning opportunity instead of drowning in shame and humiliation. Fear features an incentive not to fail, but laughter is the ultimate motivator. "A joyful heart is good medicine, but a crushed spirit dries up the bones" (Proverbs 17:22 ESV).

3. It encourages humility: Joking about your own misgivings is a great way to personally relate to others. Don't be so arrogant that you can't laugh at yourself, and you get suspicious and offended when others giggle around you. The one with the ego has Eased God Out. C. S. Lewis said, "A proud man cannot laugh because he must protect his dignity . . . but a poor and happy man laughs heartily because he gives no serious attention to his ego." "Even in laughter the heart may ache, and the end of joy may be grief" (Proverbs 14:13 ESV).

4. It can spread to others: Smiles and laughs are contagious, and working on a project with people who have a sense of humor can make the job so much easier. Workplace and family drama is toxic and can often be unhealthy. Life happens, and we all have problems. But doesn't mean letting these issues stop you from enjoying the blessings from the Lord. Have fun and enjoy life despite the devil's attempts to drag you down. Enjoy living the way God intended.

5. It keeps you grounded: Funny stories on social media or in the news have a way of putting life in perspective. If you don't find a way to insert humor into your life, you will be a miserable person. Appreciate the innocence of a child's laugh and try to be a part of that as much as possible. Children remind you that life is about the little things, and most of the time, whatever preoccupies you is not nearly as important as spending time with your kids. Stay grounded and be grateful that God also has a sense of humor, as He sometimes

demonstrates in the ways He answers your prayers. Laugh loud and laugh often.

Fans watching the game were not happy that FSU was dominating their Gamecocks. But Deion allowed them to see the reality of how laughter can take a moment in life and put it into perspective. Sure, their team lost, but it was not the end of the world. After all, it's just a game.

DAY 19
RELATIONSHIPS MAKE THE DIFFERENCE

November 27, 1993: FSU 33, UF 21
By Bethany Jett

From whom the whole body, joined and held together by every joint with which it is equipped, when each part is working properly, makes the body grow so that it builds itself up in love. —Ephesians 4:16 ESV

Fresh off the game against Notre Dame that dropped the 'Noles from No 1 to No. 2, despite the win, FSU headed to The Swamp to battle the Florida Gators for a spot in the FedEx Orange Bowl.

The Seminoles led 27-7 heading into the fourth quarter. The Gators quickly scored, bringing the game to 27-14. The crowd could taste blood. To upset the 'Noles' chance at the national title is what every rival's dreams are made of.

And then we come to what makes the legendary Ward-to-Dunn play so amazing.

First down. The ball is almost intercepted by the Gators.

Empty cups from angry fans rain down from the upper levels.

Second down. Ward's pass to Dunn fails. Incomplete.

The sound level is deafening.

Third down. Ward pitches the ball to Dunn, who grabs it and takes off, the blue-and-orange unable to take him down as he rushes toward the end zone for a Florida State T-O-U-C-H-D-O-W-N.

To this day, the Ward-to-Dunn play lives on in FSU infamy. Tomahawk Nation has it named number four of the top 100 FSU plays, not for the difficulty level but because of what was at stake. So, when you hear someone talk about the Ward-to-Dunn play, remember that the Seminoles went on to win the national championship, Ward won the Heisman, and the Seminoles beat UF . . . again.

And we pause here for a minute for a small history lesson. Dunn, one of the most notable wide receivers in FSU history, wasn't recruited as a wide receiver. Head Coach Bobby Bowden recruited Dunn to play defense. And yet it was at Dunn's insistence and perseverance to be the wide receiver he knew he could be that made all the difference.

> Now the full number of those who believed were of one heart and soul, and no one said that any of the things that belonged to him was his own, but they had everything in common. —Acts 4:32 ESV

FEAR THE SPEAR

Relationships matter, on and off the field. In life, we become like the people we hang around. We can lift each other up and spur each other on to success. The Ward-to-Dunn connection goes beyond the amazing play against the Gators.

After Warrick Dunn's mother was tragically murdered, he took a scholarship at Florida State as a freshman. When Doug

Williams (Redskins quarterback), a friend of Ward's mother, asked Dunn to watch out for Charlie, Ward took it a step further and made Dunn his roommate. "He's like my big brother," says Warrick, who would occasionally accompany Dunn with him on his trips home to Georgia.

We're called to take care of each other as fellow brothers and sisters in Christ. The early Church was an excellent role model in this regard. "There was not a needy person among them, for as many as were owners of lands or houses sold them and brought the proceeds of what was sold and laid it at the apostles' feet, and it was distributed to each as any had need" (Acts 4:34 ESV).

'NOLE NATION

When was the last time someone gave you an unexpected compliment? How did it make you feel? Here are five ways we can be a friend to someone who may need a leg up.

1. Demonstrate kindness. It can be as easy as paying for the food for the car behind you.

2. Offer encouragement. When you see someone trying their best, let them know. And when someone is falling a little short, an encouraging word can make all the difference.

3. Go the extra mile. Instead of doing what is expected, take things to the next level.

4. Pay a compliment. Most people go through their entire day, even weeks, without someone saying something nice

Del Duduit, Andy Clapp, and Bethany Jett

to them. In fact, most of the time, we hear negativity and complaints. Be the change.

5. Show grace. Things aren't always going to go our way. Give someone the same courtesy and benefit of the doubt that you are thankful that others show you.

Who can we help today? What can we do to provide where someone is lacking? The Ward-to-Dunn play was amazing, but it was the relationship off-camera that made a difference for a lifetime.

DAY 20
A PART OF A BIGGER MISSION

October 2, 1999: Florida State 51, Duke 13
By Andy Clapp

Do nothing out of rivalry or conceit, but in humility
consider others as more important than yourselves.
Everyone should look out not only for his own interests, but also for the interests of others. —Philippians
2:3–4 HCSB

A winless Duke team traveled to Jacksonville to face the
top-ranked, undefeated Seminoles. The game quickly turned
into a rout.

On the third play from scrimmage, Brian Allen made a
juggling interception to give FSU the ball on the Duke side of
the field. Eight plays later, Chris Weinke hit Peter Warrick for
a touchdown.

Neither Warrick nor Weinke was finished. Midway through
the first quarter, Weinke flipped the ball out to Warrick on a
short route. Warrick took the ball in, turned on the speed,
and headed to the end zone. Thanks to a block by Laveranues
Coles, Warrick reached the end zone for the second time in
the opening quarter, giving the Seminoles a 14-0 lead. Another
two-yard toss from Weinke to Warrick less than four minutes
later gave the duo three touchdowns in one quarter.

Sebastian Janikowski kicked two field goals before Peter Warrick struck again. With the ball at the Duke 35, Warrick lined up at quarterback and threw a 35-yard touchdown to Laveranues Coles, giving the Seminoles a commanding 34-0 lead.

Just over halfway through the second quarter, Weinke rolled out again and tossed the ball toward the end zone. Dan Kendra, the former quarterback whose career was derailed by an injury, hauled in the pass and bowled over Blue Devil defenders to reach the end zone. The now fullback raised his arms in celebration as the 'Noles expanded the lead to 41-0.

Duke logged 13 unanswered points against the reserves before Coach Bowden put Weinke back in to slam the door on any thoughts the Blue Devils had of a comeback.

Duke scampered back to Durham, North Carolina, with another loss while the Seminoles told the world they were on a mission.

> The life I now live in the body, I live by faith in the
> Son of God, who loved me and gave Himself for me.
> —Galatians 2:20 HCSB

FEAR THE SPEAR

We lay out plans for an entire section of our life. Your planner holds the master design for the upcoming week. High School is a preparation for the college we long to attend. College years provide knowledge for a career. Five-year goals and retirement goals dictate our trajectory. A ten-year plan pushes you to complete certain goals in a decade. But what do we do when the dreams are dashed or derailed completely? What do we do when plans change or our abilities are taken away completely? Dan Kendra planned to be the quarterback, but after a devastating injury, he faced a decision. Rather than quit, he adapted to a new role on the team to help the Seminoles win a second national championship.

'NOLE NATION

Dan Kendra's story teaches us a larger lesson in life. Life features twists and turns, some of which alter all that we had planned prior. Simply quitting on the cause when life shifts should not be an option. Kendra played to win, regardless of the position or the notoriety.

All of us can contribute in some way. Of course, not all will be in the limelight, but the humility inside the heart of any Christian should be to serve in any role, regardless of whether it is seen by others or only seen by the Lord.

As Paul wrote to the Philippians, he focused the believers on what they could do and what they should do. He instructed that they see others as more than themselves and to look out for the needs of others rather than only focusing on their own needs. What Paul taught was for the believers in Philippi to be part of something bigger. He implored a life of humility that produces righteous results. He taught them to have the same mentality as Jesus, giving of themselves.

As Christians, we are all part of the same team, and ultimately, what we are called to accomplish for the kingdom is bigger than any one of us. We strive for His glory. We take part in what is His story. When we see the beauty of being a part of something bigger, we relish in the fact that we are any part of that story. Our passion for Him pushes us to be willing to do anything He calls us to do, even if it is a far cry from what we originally had in mind.

Here are a few ways to step up and take your place in the Lord's work today:

1. Humility marks an effective servant—humility prepares us to take on any role that leads us to victory. Humility marked the attitude of Christ as we read in Philippians 2:8.

2. See the effectiveness of multiple people coming together—more is accomplished when more are involved. Being a part of God's team means you have an army by your side as you help to carry out His plan.

3. Know that He sees—the Lord's eyes are always on us. Though the role you have may attract less attention in the eyes of the world, He is always paying attention, seeing every contribution we make.

4. Do what you do well—excel in whatever your role may be. The effort to excel matters in everything we do. What you are doing is an offering to the Lord, so do it well.

5. Remember who receives the glory—when it is all about the glory of God, we work and point to the Lord. When we find success, it's His success. When we overcome, it is because He overcomes.

Dan Kendra's story teaches us to lace up the cleats and get in the game, no matter the position we are called to take. Kendra helped his team to a championship. Though it was not the way he originally thought it would be, a ring still signifies his part in winning it all.

DAY 21

USING OUR GIFTS

November 21, 1998: FSU 23, UF 12
By Bethany Jett

The eye cannot say to the hand, "I have no need of you,"
nor again the head to the feet, "I have no need of you." . . .
If one member suffers, all suffer together; if one member
is honored, all rejoice together." —1 Corinthians 12:21,
26 ESV

Traditionally played the Saturday after Thanksgiving, this
rivalry matchup was the last game for this FSU season. The No.
5 'Noles were 10-1 and needed this win to move forward for
a shot at the national title. Unfortunately, quarterback Chris
Weinke's injury during the game against Virginia two weeks
prior meant quarterback Marcus Outzen had the pleasure of
leading the team to victory.

The offense struggled early on, with the only points added
to FSU's scoreboard were from kicker Sebastian Janikowski.
Then the 'Noles got creative and put on a display of incredible
athleticism that showcased the many gifts of their star running
back Peter Warrick.

After scoring a touchdown of his own in the third quarter,
Warrick threw a 46-yard touchdown pass to Ron Dugans to
seal the win.

Florida State secured its spot for the national championship *and*, most important, defeated the Gators.

> As each has received a gift, use it to serve one another, as good stewards of God's varied grace. —1 Peter 4:10 ESV

FEAR THE SPEAR

Warrick's athleticism was showcased in his ability to play (albeit temporarily) a position that he wasn't well-known for. But, he saw the opportunity and took it. And boy, did it ever pay off.

God has given us all unique gifts, but sometimes we may have a hard time figuring out what ours are. If you're unsure where your true passion lies, experiment in the areas where you have a knack or genuine interest until you figure out where your talent, strengths, and interests are best utilized.

And remember, you can be good at more than one thing. We aren't confined to one talent or one skill. In fact, Jesus shared a parable about talents. In Matthew 25, we meet three servants who are entrusted with their master's property: five talents were given to one man, two talents to the second, and one talent to the third. The first two servants used their talents to gain more, thus increasing the master's wealth, but the third buried his.

While it may have felt too risky to lose the only talent he'd be given, Jesus did not see it that way. Instead, the master shamed the man who buried the talent, telling him that, at the very least, he could have gained interest by putting the money in the bank.

Our lesson, therefore, is with the servants who were able to provide an increase. "You have been faithful over a little; I will set you over much" (Matthew 25:23).

'NOLE NATION

I don't know about you, but I don't want to be like the servant who buried the talent. Part of me understands why he was afraid of losing the only talent he had. However, it's clear that God expects us to use our gifts because He gave them to us. We aren't to hide them, even if we're not sure how best to utilize them. So that we don't become like the shamed servant, here are five ways to use our gifts to the best of our availability:

1. Step out of your comfort zone. How will you know what you're good at unless you try your hand and different things?

2. Practice. We're not experts immediately. The more time and energy we invest, the better the results.

3. Start where you are and use what you have. Everyone who has ever succeeded started somewhere. For instance, the company Apple started in a garage, Starbucks was founded by three teachers who sold coffee beans, and Kentucky Fried Chicken was birthed by sixty-year-old Harland Sanders, who sold his chicken at a service station.

4. Don't diminish your gifts. God gave you special talents to use, and you shouldn't apologize for them. If you can sing, praise His name through your music. If you're

artistically inclined, paint or draw and bring Him glory. And if you can write, use your words to bring others to His word.

5. Know that sometimes you won't see the effects of your gifts. Some of us plant, some water, but it is God who brings the growth—in His timing.

6. Follow your purpose and passions because we each have a part to play in furthering God's kingdom.

While it's important to play our roles, we can't *not* play our part. Have you put yourself into a box? Have you been afraid to step out when an opportunity presents itself because it's not what you consider to be your role? Let today be the day that you grab the next chance that comes your way.

DAY 22
TRADITIONS ARE IMPORTANT

FSU Culture: Game Day Traditions
By Bethany Jett

Therefore, since we are surrounded by so great a cloud of witnesses, let us also lay aside every weight, and sin which clings so closely, and let us run with endurance the race that is set before us. —Hebrews 12:1 ESV

The roar of the crowd is nothing compared to the sounds and atmosphere of the Florida State student section. The party starts early on game days with tailgating outside the stadium and with frat houses and collegiate clubs gathering pregame on campus.

By the time Chief Osceola and Renegade prance onto the field, fiery spear ready to be thrown into the 50-yard-line center, the air is charged with college students ready to chop to the war chant and yell their way to a F-L-O-R-I-D-A S-T-A-T-E victory.

The student section view may not be the clear, see-the-whole-field seating experience, but you've got a front-row seat to the super sparkly Garnet & Gold Guys, a special tradition of the Baptist Collegiate Ministry.

While you're in the stands, you'll dance to the incredible sounds and dancing of the Marching Chiefs drumline. Once a season, the entire campus will be filled with the sounds of the

Chiefs as they perform the annual Campus Crawl to hype up the student body.

And if you're lucky enough to be on campus the night *before* a home game, head past Langford Green to check out the Unconquered statue on the south side of the stadium. The thirty-one-foot-high spear-wielding Seminole tribe member atop a rearing horse will have the tip of the spear lit on fire at sunset.

> Remember the former things of old; for I am God, and there is no other; I am God, and there is none like me.
> —Isaiah 46:9 ESV

FEAR THE SPEAR

While different denominations practice different traditions of their faith, we have to remember not to confuse tradition with biblical disciplines. For example, in the Gospel of Mark, Jesus says that the Jews rejected the commands of God in favor of their own traditions (Mark 7). Additionally, Paul talks about tradition becoming religion and the zealousness of traditions (see Galatians 1:14).

While we may not practice certain traditions, there are underlying spiritual disciplines that can be followed? As an example, some believers may not celebrate Lent, but the practice of giving things up to grow closer to God. Likewise, during Advent, the focus is on the birth of Christ, which is the point of Christmas in the first place.

'NOLE NATION

Scholars have categorized spiritual disciplines in a couple of ways. Some divide them into three groups (inward, outward, and corporate), while others break them down into two (abstinence and engagement).

While there are several spiritual disciplines, here are five that we can put into practice:

1. Prayer. When praying becomes rote, only at meals and bedtimes, it's time to get on our knees and spend meaningful time in prayer with our heavenly Father.

2. Meditation and memorization. The scripture says we should meditate on God's word, day and night (see Joshua 1:8). The practice of memorization can be easily neglected, but it's vital for us to fill our minds and hearts with His word.

3. Fasting. The purpose of fasting is to temporarily deny our physical needs while using that time to seek God. Many times, fasting will be done to ensure we're hearing God's voice.

4. Solitude. Jesus demonstrated this discipline several times in the scriptures. He often went off by himself, pairing the discipline of solitude with other disciplines. Jesus prayed by Himself many times, and when He went to the desert for forty days, we see Him practicing the spiritual discipline of fasting, as well.

5. Silence. The Bible says to "be still and know that I am God" (see Psalm 40:6). The practice of silence is to quiet our spirits so that we can better listen and hear from God.

Del Duduit, Andy Clapp, and Bethany Jett

As we are reminded in Hebrews, we are surrounded by a great cloud of witnesses, the saints that came before. Let us utilize their example, as well as that of Jesus Christ our Lord, and apply the spiritual disciplines to our lives so that we can also fight the good fight and run the ultimate race.

96

DAY 23
MAKE THE COMEBACK

September 22, 2012: Florida State 49, Clemson 37
By Del Duduit

For I know the plans I have for you, declares the LORD,
plans for welfare and not for evil, to give you a future
and a hope. —Jeremiah 29:11 ESV

Clemson took an early lead in the game between two Top 10
teams and posted a 21-14 advantage at the half. The Tigers
picked up where they left off in the third quarter when they
extended the lead to 28-14 after a touchdown pass from
quarterback Tajh Boyd to Andre Ellington.

By this time, the Seminoles and quarterback E. J. Manuel
had had enough from Clemson. The next four FSU possessions
resulted in TDs. Manuel threw for a career-high 380 yards and
two touchdowns and added 102 yards on the ground to lead a
massive comeback win.

Running back Chris Thompson added 104 yards rushing
with a pair of scores, while James Wilder Jr. contributed two
touchdowns of his own to the victory.

Can you make a comeback when things are going your way?

Behold, the days are coming, declares the LORD, when
I will make a new covenant with the house of Israel
and the house of Judah, not like the covenant that I

made with their fathers on the day when I took them by the hand to bring them out of the land of Egypt, my covenant that they broke, though I was their husband, declares the LORD. But this is the covenant that I will make with the house of Israel after those days, declares the LORD: I will put my law within them, and I will write it on their hearts. And I will be their God, and they shall be my people. And no longer shall each one teach his neighbor and each his brother, saying, 'Know the LORD,' for they shall all know me, from the least of them to the greatest, declares the LORD. For I will forgive their iniquity, and I will remember their sin no more. —Jeremiah 31:31–34 ESV

FEAR THE SPEAR

Have you found yourself down by a large deficit in the game of life? Perhaps you have suffered the consequences of addiction or lost a job you thought would have until retirement. Or maybe a long-trusted friend has turned his back on you and betrayed your confidence. Can you remember a time when the enemy posted what seemed to be an insurmountable lead over you? Perhaps someone you looked up to in authority in the church has fallen, or you have lost a friend because of a wrong you committed. No matter who might be at fault, you may have allowed the enemy to take a big lead, and this has caused you to drift away from your faith and the Lord.

'NOLE NATION

Everyone can make a mistake that could lead to a spiritual setback. Even you. No one is above God's law, and we "all have sinned, and fall short of the glory of God" (Romans 3:23 ESV). This is exactly why Jesus was born of a virgin, was crucified, and rose again from the dead—to take away our sins and provide us with the opportunity to live with Him forever. But you must make a comeback and find your way back to the cross. One of the best things you can do is be vigilant about your spiritual condition and prevent the devil from posting a big lead on you in the first half. Here are some warning signs that you may be falling behind.

1. When your church attendance slips: This tells everyone who knows you that something is wrong. If you are upset with a fellow church member and decide to protest by not showing up, you are only hurting yourself. You should never let someone else interfere with the relationship between you and God. Nothing is worth sacrificing fellowship with your brothers and sisters in Christ. You need to be in church faithfully to praise Christ for what He has done for you. "So faith comes from hearing, and hearing through the word of Christ" (Romans 10:17 ESV).

2. When you stop reading God's word: You might tell yourself that you don't have enough time to read the Bible, but you know this is not the real reason. You find time for what you want to do, which is an issue of the heart. If you can carve out a few minutes to post on social media, then you can also read a few passages of scripture. When you fall away from reading the Bible, you have a spiritual problem that needs to be addressed right away. It's not your neighbor's issue. It is yours.

3. When your prayer life slows down: Would you go a few days without speaking to your spouse, kids, parents, or friends? No, because your relationship would suffer. When you stop praying, do you take into consideration how God feels? He loves to hear from His children, and daily communication with Him is vital to your Christian walk.

4. When you judge others: You are responsible for your actions. When you let your feelings about other people come between you and your relationship with the heavenly Father, this is a warning sign that you have some word to do in your spiritual life. No matter what someone may have said about you or done to you, let God deal with it, and don't let it impact your spiritual condition. When Judgment Day comes, you are only responsible for yourself. "My little children, I am writing these things to you so that you may not sin. But if anyone does sin, we have an advocate with the Father, Jesus Christ the righteous" (1 John 2:1 ESV).

5. When you become bitter: Bitterness, when left to simmer, will cause physical, mental, emotional, and spiritual damage. Forgiveness is a much easier road to travel than hatred toward another person. "Let all bitterness and wrath and anger and clamor and slander be put away from you, along with all malice" (Ephesians 4:31 ESV).

The 'Noles made a comeback for the ages. Clemson might have thought the game was in the bag going into the third quarter. But Manuel and his team had other plans. They banded together as a team and made the charge to win. Take note of your spiritual condition, and don't find yourself down by a large margin with a few minutes left in the game. Know that God will always make a way for you to come back to Him for the victory.

DAY 24
OVERCOMING THE ODDS

November 29, 2003: FSU 38, UF 34
By Bethany Jett

Now to him who is able to do far more abundantly than all that we ask or think, according to the power at work within us, to him be glory in the church and in Christ Jesus throughout all generations, forever and ever. Amen. ——Ephesians 3:20–21 ESV

If there was ever a game to solidify the intense loathing between the No. 9 Florida State Seminoles and the No. 11 University of Florida Gators, the 2003 matchup affectionately known as "The Swindle in the Swamp" might take the proverbial cake.

After defeating UF the year prior in Tallahassee, it was time to defeat the Gators on their swampy home turf.

Even before the first play, a fight almost broke out at midfield, a sign of the tense moments to come. The game was littered with questionable calls from Atlantic Coast Conference (ACC) refs that left fans angry. After the game, the police had to escort the officials off the field for their safety.

Anything can happen in a rivalry game. Near the end of the fourth quarter, down by 3, with less than a minute remaining, the 'Noles faced an unfortunate reality. They were on the fourth down with 14 yards to the line of scrimmage.

Fourth and 4.

103

Down by three.

In the fourth quarter.

Not great odds.

But the 'Noles have a reputation for fourth-quarter comebacks, and this game was no exception. First, Chris Rix hit Dominic Robinson for a key first down at the 'Noles 48. Then, with the seconds ticking down, Rix connected with P. K. Sam for a 52-yard game-winning touchdown with fifty-five seconds left.

What a complete 180-degree turn for the 'Noles!

Interestingly, in 2020, Florida State found themselves in another fourth and 14 with their other rival, the University of Miami Hurricanes. Out of field goal range, the 'Noles needed a big pass. So quarterback Jordan Travis threw to Andrew Parchment, who ran the ball to the one-yard line, with Travis sneaking the ball in on the next play with twenty-six seconds left for a 31-28 win.

The 2003 "Swindle in the Swamp" and the 2021 Miami moments are memorialized in FSU fandom with Travis's launch of licensed T-shirts bearing his signature and the phrase "4th and 14."

Love bears all things, believes all things, hopes all things, endures all things. —1 Corinthians 13:7 ESV

FEAR THE SPEAR

There is a lot of trust required when going into a 4th and 14 situation. The odds are against you, and you're running out of time. In FSU's case, the quarterback trusts that the line will hold up. Next, he trusts that he'll read the field correctly and throw the ball to the right spot at the right time. Finally, he trusts that his receiver will catch the ball.

Likewise, in times of trial, we must trust our team, our family, and our inner circle. Just like Jesus had his inner circle of Peter, James, and John, it's important for us to cultivate relationships that are strong and rooted in Christ. And if you're in a stage of life where you don't have an inner circle, it's time to get on your knees and ask God to bring them to you.

'NOLE NATION

When was the last time you felt like you were making last-minute decisions that could change the course of your future? Who did you have to depend on to ensure success? Here are five ways to show perseverance under incredible odds:

1. Remember that you're not alone. Others have been in your situation and have overcome the odds. If you're not part of a local church, find one. Look up faith-based groups online and start joining the conversation. There are people out there ready to be your friend. Sometimes, we have to put the work into finding them.

2. Build deep relationships. Invest in other people. Ask about their day. Listen to their concerns. Help where you can. Be there when they need someone.

3. Humble yourself. Serving others is an excellent way for God to change your perspective on a situation.

4. Position yourself to lead effectively. Knowing how to support those around is just as important as having people there to help you when you're down.

5. Give it your all. Once you've done your part, you have to let go and trust that God is in control.

The truth is—our mission is not won or lost by ourselves. Life takes a team, a family, and a peer group, all supporting each other. When we don't know where else to turn, sometimes we have to look outside of ourselves and throw a pass to a teammate, trusting that they'll have our back and can help us reach the collective goal.

DAY 25
SEIZE THE OPPORTUNITY BEFORE YOU

January 1, 1994: Florida State 18, Nebraska 16
By Andy Clapp

Teach us to number our days carefully so that we may
develop wisdom in our hearts. —Psalm 90:12 HCSB

Sixty minutes separated two legendary coaches from their
first national championship. Tom Osborne of Nebraska nearly
won at the end of the 1983 season. Bobby Bowden fell victim
to missed field goals in previous seasons that kept him from
hoisting the trophy. At the end of New Year's Day 1994, one
would be called national champion.

The 'Noles were favored by more than two touchdowns,
but the Nebraska defense swarmed the Seminole offense to
keep the scoring low.

The thought of "here we go again" swept through the 'Nole
Nation as Scott Bentley missed his first field goal attempt. He
connected on two field goals in the first half, but Nebraska led
going into the locker room, 7-6.

FSU took the lead in the third quarter as William Floyd
blasted his way into the end zone. Though he fumbled at the
goal line, the officials ruled it a touchdown. Another Bentley
field goal pushed the lead to 15-7, still too close for comfort.

The Cornhuskers struck in the fourth quarter. Lawrence
Phillips reached the end zone to cut into the deficit. The

Huskers tried for two but missed, leaving them behind, 15-13. With just over one minute left to play in the game, Nebraska added a field goal to take the lead.

FSU's Heisman Trophy quarterback Charlie Ward wanted another trophy. He led the 'Noles down the field, aided by costly penalties. Freshman Scott Bentley took the field and kicked the game winner with only twenty-one seconds to play.

Though Nebraska had a shot at winning, their long field goal attempt sailed wide left, giving the Seminoles their first national championship.

> You don't even know what tomorrow will bring—what your life will be! For you are like smoke that appears for a little while, then vanishes. —James 4:14 HCSB

FEAR THE SPEAR

There stands a once-in-a-lifetime opportunity. Today, you can lay hold to your dreams, or you can let this chance pass by in the hopes that it will come around again. This moment presents the opportunity for you to take charge and take the next step in your faith, in your life, or even in your career today. Don't let it pass you by because you are not guaranteed that you will have another chance tomorrow. Too often, we are lulled to sleep by the lie that there will always be more time.

'NOLE NATION

Just as the 'Noles waited for that moment in the Orange Bowl, the national championship game where a win guaranteed them the ultimate prize, you have waited for a chance to take the next step in your life. Now, it's here. It is up to you to take it. Today is an opportunity, and outside of this very moment, we have no guarantees we will have another chance.

The psalms teach us so much, and one of the key truths comes from Psalm 90. The writer implores the Lord to teach him of the fleeting nature of life. As each day passes, we are one breath closer to eternity. The psalmist asks for perspective in the hopes of developing wisdom as a result.

The psalmist teaches us that there is a set amount of time on earth, and it should be used wisely. Rather than seeing time and opportunity as endless, we must see both as limited and take advantage of the opportunities before us. Take the chance to advance. Grab the moment and make the most of it.

Bobby Bowden didn't want to be the greatest coach to never win a championship. Years of close calls made the moment of the Orange Bowl even more meaningful for the Seminoles and their leader. The drive for greatness pushes us to embrace and make the most of today's opportunity. Do you want to excel? Make it happen today instead of hoping for tomorrow.

All of life features a next-step opportunity. From crawling to walking, high school to college, career to retirement, progressions take place. So, take the leap forward today instead of assuming you can do so later.

Here are some truths to help you seize the opportunity of this moment you have been given:

1. Today is your guarantee—the psalmist said our days were numbered and limited. James wrote that we don't know what tomorrow will bring. Today holds a championship moment in your life. Wisely make the most of the day.

2. Growth today brings benefits tomorrow—every opportunity seized today will provide benefits tomorrow and beyond. Don't waste the day when you can launch your life forward.

3. Take the reins of your dreams—dreams without action are nothing more than daydreams. Seize this day as a chance to make your life's dreams a reality.

4. See the opportunity as a one-shot only opportunity—too often, we believe the same chances will come around again. There are no guarantees. When you see an opportunity as a single chance, you'll give it all you have.

5. Don't forget what got you to today—the work that was put in yesterday leads us to today's opportunities. Don't forget what you've gone through to get here—make the most of today, remembering all of the sacrifices of yesterday.

Bobby Bowden and the Seminoles took advantage of the moment. They won the game and earned the championship trophy. Rather than hope they'd get another shot, they made the most of the guaranteed shot they had against Nebraska.

DAY 26
DOWN TO THE "WIRE-TO-WIRE"

January 4, 2000: FSU 46, Virginia Tech 29
By Bethany Jett

Whatever your hand finds to do, do it with your might.
—Ecclesiastes 9:10 ESV

The 1999 Sugar Bowl brought an immense amount of pressure to Florida State. Not only was the national championship title on the line, but the team was also playing for a record-breaking season.

Before the playoff system, polling determined who won the national championship game. Sunday morning papers were flung open to the sports section to check the rankings. The 1999 season was *the* season for Florida State fans.

The 'Noles started the season as No. 1 in the Associated Press poll and continued their streak as No. 1 each week. The Sugar Bowl would determine if FSU would pull off this never-been-done-before feat.

Quarterback Chris Weinke, who sat out the previous year's championship game because of a neck injury, said, "This is something I was waiting for. . . . We said last year we could go wire-to-wire and when we went down in the third quarter, we responded."[3]

---

[3] Associated Press, "It's Wire-to-Wire as FSU Wins Title," Ironton (OH) Tribune, January 5, 2000, https://www.irontontribune.com/2000/01/05/its-wire-to-wire-as-fsu-wins-title/.

Respond, they did.

The team played their hearts out against the Hokies, with Peter Warrick winning the Most Outstanding Player award and securing the Sugar Bowl record for points. The game ended with the 'Noles boasting an impressive 46 points over Virginia Tech's 29, giving them bragging rights and the impressive distinction of being the first ever Wire-to-Wire winners.

To sweeten the pot, the 'Noles gave Head Coach Bobby Bowden his first ever undefeated season.

But the 'Noles did more than show up. They walked the walk during the season, day in and day out. Imagine how much pressure it takes to make sure all the little things are right: workouts. Water. Healthy food. Sleep. Practice. Practice. Practice.

The hard work, dedication, and perseverance of the 'Noles paid off . . . all the way to their second national championship title.

What you have learned and received and heard and seen in me—practice these things, and the God of peace will be with you. —Philippians 4:9 ESV

FEAR THE SPEAR

"Don't practice until you get it right. Practice until you can't get it wrong,"[4] is an oft-used quote by coaches and is a motto that can benefit us in so many areas of life. What we see in the 'Noles' 1999 season and the championship title that followed is that hard work pays off. What we don't see is the sweat, blood, and tears it took to get them there.

---

[4] Attributed to multiple authors, including Ziad K. Abdelnour; McKayla Maroney; John Flanagan.

How many times have we given up on a dream because it feels insurmountable? The year prior, the 'Noles lost the national championship to Tennessee, but they rebounded and came back stronger than ever.

Psalm 30:5 says, "Weeping may tarry for the night, but joy comes with the morning" (ESV). This verse is often used for encouragement during difficult seasons but let's focus on the second part of the verse: Joy comes with the morning.

There is hope.

A new day is coming.

'NOLE NATION

Here are five ways we can demonstrate our trustworthiness, dedication, and perseverance in the small things:

1. Take your time. My husband often says, "Slow is steady, and steady is fast." Mistakes happen when we rush, so practicing discipline allows for better results.

2. Eliminate negative voices. Sometimes the people closest to us are the naysayers when we want to venture out and do something new. Most of the time, their caution is because they want to protect us.

3. Ask God for discernment. It's important to know when a negative voice should be listened to. Ignore those who spew hate and ugliness, love those who are trying to protect you, and listen to those who are wiser and may be keeping you from making a bad decision.

4. Surround yourself with people with similar goals. We become like the people we hang around, so find those with a similar work ethic.

5. Do all things with a cheerful attitude. It's OK to be disappointed when things go wrong, but we can learn, pivot, and do better on the next go around.

We may not be the national championship winners, but we can apply their dedication to our own lives by pursuing our purpose with excellence, knowing that even the tasks that are overlooked by others are always seen by God.

DAY 27
FINISH IT WELL

January 1, 2010: Florida State 33, West Virginia 21
By Andy Clapp

Don't you know that the runners in a stadium all race,
but only one receives the prize. Run in such a way to
win the prize. —1 Corinthians 9:24 HCSB

Everything here on earth comes to an end.

The 'Noles finished the 2009 season with an invitation to play the West Virginia Mountaineers in the Gator Bowl. Bobby Bowden took the field for his final game coaching against the team he formerly coached.

The Mountaineers threatened to spoil Bowden's sendoff, striking with big plays in the first quarter. Quarterback Jarrett Brown ran the ball in from 32 yards out for the first score of the game. On the second possession for WVU, Noel Devine dashed down the sideline for a seventy-yard gain. Moments later, Devine carried it in from the one-yard line, putting the Mountaineers up 14-3.

Early in the second quarter, Florida State's Dustin Hopkins missed a field goal, a tragic reminder of painful losses from the past.

An interception, however, turned the tide. Jamie Robinson's pick injected new life into the men from Tallahassee. The 'Noles drove down the field, and Jermaine Thomas scored on a 12-yard run. Hopkins connected on a field goal just before the half to pull FSU to within one at the break, 14-13.

Coming out after halftime, the 'Noles snagged the lead and never let go of it. Determined to send Coach Bowden off with a victory, Greg Reid took the opening kickoff 69 yards, which led to a field goal. Later in the third, Thomas scored his second touchdown of the Gator Bowl.

When West Virginia scored to open the fourth quarter and cut into the Seminoles' lead, 23-21, E. J. Manuel drove the 'Noles methodically down the field. His touchdown made it a two-score game again. Hopkins put the game away with a final field goal.

The epitome of a champion, Coach Bowden went out as one. Not just on the field but also in life.

I have fought the good fight, I have finished the race, I have kept the faith. —2 Timothy 4:7 HCSB

FEAR THE SPEAR

You can ride it out, cruising on past accomplishments as sufficient enough. Going through the motions tempts you as the end of a particular season in your life draws closer. In your mind, you can justify doing the bare minimum, and you may even hear others say that they wouldn't blame you if you mailed it in. But there is merit in rising above such a mentality. Maybe we should finish it well, regardless of what's happening around us. The legacy of ending well leaves an impact on those who follow in our footsteps. Ending well provides positive momentum for all those involved.

'NOLE NATION

As Bobby Bowden neared the end of his time at Florida State, controversy surrounded his departure. Some believed he was being forced out and should leave when he said it was time. However, Bobby led the team with the same passion regardless of what was happening around him.

Paul implored the Corinthians to live well to the end. They had started the race of faith, and they'd run hard. But they had to continue to run it until the end, staying the course along the way. Paul's analogy was that of a competition, complete with a beginning and an end. The end is just as critical as the beginning.

Paul told them to run in a way that would win the prize. To do so, they had to finish the race they began. Their original passion had to propel them to the end. How far they had come did not outweigh how much further they had to go.

Life offers us a multitude of reasons and opportunities to mail it in, especially after we've seemingly accomplished so much. Cruising to the close and going on with life serves as an enticement to reward ourselves for what we have already done. But finishing well is highly important. Of all the highlights of yesterday, there is a lasting image that others will carry with them. Of all the things we remember, we recall how things end. Stories are told about the last stand, the final fall when the champion is knocked out, and the horrible breakup and fallout after that. But that can be avoided by finishing well. Here are a few things to consider as you work to finish well:

1. Leave a legacy—Give people something worth remembering because you dedicate yourself to finishing well. Take no shortcuts. Think about the last image that will be carried beyond your last day.

2. Finish well for the sake of others—Finishing well impacts not only us but those around us. Bobby Bowden had a team of eighty-five players who needed him to give his best. We have others that need us to finish well too.

3. Keep who you've been intact—Even if the ending of the season of your life is happening on someone else's terms, keep your testimony intact. Refuse to damage your legacy with words or actions that are outside the character others have witnessed in you.

4. Set the standard for others to follow—Any standard that we set should be one the next person should want to attain and build from. One coach sets a standard for the next. Identify how to set the right standard in your life and how you finish.

5. Finish with another victory—Propel yourself to go out on top. That desire alone will help you to finish well.

When Bobby Bowden took the field the final time to start the game, he planted the spear at midfield. By game's end, Florida State's greatest coach had won his twenty-first bowl game and finished with another winning record. So finish everything well because finishing well sets the tone for those who come next.

DAY 28
STIFF-ARM SATAN'S TACKLE

October 12, 1985: Auburn 59, Florida State 27
By Del Duduit

Therefore, submit to God. Resist the devil and he will flee from you. —James 4:7 ESV

The buzz was everywhere. Two of the greatest athletes to play college and professional football matched up on October 12, 1988, at Jordan-Hare Stadium in Alabama in front of 75,000 fans.

Bo Jackson, a powerhouse running back for No. 12-ranked Auburn, faced off against a talented freshman defensive corner-back at FSU named Deion Sanders. The two dominated college football at their positions and later took the NFL by storm, and both eventually even played Major League Baseball.

But before there was "Prime Time," Sanders got a lesson in humility because "Bo Knows" stiff-arms.

Undefeated Florida State (4-0) rolled into Auburn with hopes of leaping into the top two with a win.

But Bo had other plans.

The Tigers took it to the 'Noles and won, 59-27.

But that is not all that everyone remembers about this game. One moment will live on forever.

Jackson took the ball on the 35-yard line and came hard around the left side. Then, he dashed through the hole and was off to the races.

Sanders, as only he could, later described the play and what happened to him on the *Dan Patrick Show*. "Bo goes into the huddle at Auburn and throws his hands up as if he's signifying the crowd to get it up," he said.

They start cheering and applauding. I was playing left corner. Bo got a sweep to his left away from me and hit it. I mean, hit it. He was gone. I came out of nowhere because I could fly. Came and got him. Ran up on him like it was no other. With his right arm, he extended it and placed it on my helmet as if he's praying for me. Palming my helmet and stiffed me down and kept going into the end zone like I wasn't even there. That was my Bo Jackson moment.

Jackson used the stiff-arm to perfection to protect himself from being tackled. When executed correctly, the move can fend off even the best defenders.

To make the move count, the player who administers the stiff-arm needs to be strong and have good hand-eye coordination. The force from the arm in a downward move shoves the defender to the turf.

The Heisman Trophy statue actually depicts a running back preparing to use the move to perfection.

When you see the devil coming from behind to take you down, are you ready to apply the stiff-arm?

Nor give place to the devil. —Ephesians 4:27 NKJV

FEAR THE SPEAR

You might be strong in the Lord, attend church on a regular basis, pray, and read your Bible. You might even hold an office at your church and be considered a person of integrity. But then, without notice, the forces of evil come at you hard. They see an opening and go throw the line right at you. This can be in the form of an outright lie or a past sin that is exposed. How is your spiritual strength? Can you avoid the blitz and get out of the way, or will you get run over and tackled? How will you fend off the attacks from the devil?

'NOLE NATION

One thing is certain. You cannot fight Satan alone, and you must depend on the Lord to provide blockers for protection. So, when the enemy runs up to you and tries to bring you down through temptations, health issues, mistruths, job losses, or relationship breakups, will you let him take you to the turf, or will you use godly tools to fend him off? Here are some ways you can stiff-arm the devil.

1. Rebuke him with faith and prayer: When the devil comes at you, the best way to defend yourself is to say the name of Jesus and tell the devil to get lost. Satan is afraid of the Lord, and when he picks on a child of God, you must call on reinforcements and call on the Savior's name.

2. Praise your way through it: Bo raised his arms and asked for the support of the fans at Auburn. And it worked. The same goes for you. When you are about to come out of the life's huddle, raise your hands and praise the Lord. Even if you get stopped for a short gain, give God the

glory. When you can praise God for the small yardage, just imagine how much you will celebrate when you go the distance for the score. "For the LORD is great and greatly to be praised; He is also to be feared above all gods" (1 Chronicles 16:25 NKJV).

3. Quote scripture or a song: If the devil fills you with fear, one way to stiff-arm is to repeat a favorite verse or sing a gospel song that provides encouragement. This will give you confidence and peace when you need it the most.

4. Realize your weaknesses: You cannot allow pride to get in the way when the devil comes at you. You must submit and call on the Lord to help you or reach out and ask a Christian friend to hold you up in prayer. Like the song from Sunday school says, "We are weak, but He is strong." "The LORD is my strength and song, And He has become my salvation; He is my God, and I will praise Him; My father's God, and I will exalt Him" (Exodus 15:2 NKJV).

5. Look at the scoreboard: This should be a go-to move for all believers. When Satan is ready to make a move to tackle you for the loss, remember who wins in the end. God's word is true, and you should look forward to the day when Satan is defeated forever.

Jackson used the move to toss Sanders to the ground and go on for the score. You can do the same and ask Jesus in His name to cast the devil out of your situation.

DAY 29
STRENGTH THROUGH WEAKNESS

November 27, 2010: FSU 31, UF 7
By Bethany Jett

But he said to me, "My grace is sufficient for you, for my power is made perfect in weakness."Therefore, I will boast all the more gladly of my weaknesses, so that the power of Christ may rest upon me. —2 Corinthians 12:9 ESV

The FSU-UF rivalry game streak reached six losses for the 'Noles from 2004 to 2009. To make matters worse for the FSU faithful, the Gators also boasted national championships under Tim Tebow and Chris Leak.

With Bobby Bowden's retirement in 2009, an era opened for new Head Coach Jimbo Fisher. The 2010 game was his first meeting with the Gators and coaching against their long-standing coach Urban Meyer.

Despite the Gators' recent success, many FSU fans felt this was the year to end the losing streak.

"For me personally, for the seniors, it was emotional because it was our last game in Doak Campbell, our last game to have a chance to beat Florida," said Christian Ponder.[5]

---

[5] Corey Clark, "War Chant: Ponder Looks Back on FSU's Streak-Breaking Win over UF in 2010,"Warchant.com, June 10, 2020, https://floridas-tate.rivals.com/news/war-chat-ponder-looks-back-on-fsu-s-streak-break-ing-win-over-uf-in-2010.

The entire team gave it their all, but props go to Christian Ponder, who was suffering an elbow injury that required five hundred ccs of fluid to be removed after their game against North Carolina three weeks before the UF game. For perspective, that's a cringeworthy amount, equaling around two cups or one-fourth of a two-liter bottle.

But there is strength in weakness, and the 'Noles rallied against their state rival.

The Seminole defense was a force to be reckoned with. After UF's first touchdown early in the game, the 'Noles didn't allow any more points the rest of the game.

As Ponder ran off the field to the locker room at halftime, he threw a cheeky Gator chomp to the Florida State student section and disappeared in the tunnel to the roar of the crowd. The second half was no picnic for the Gators, particularly with Ponder's third-quarter touchdown pass that landed beautifully in the hands of Willie Haulstead.

The much-needed win ended the losing streak, and Jimbo Fisher celebrated the first of many wins against the rival Gators.

You give us victory over our enemies, you put our adversaries to shame. —Psalm 44:7 NIV

FEAR THE SPEAR

God uses the weak to shame the strong. Think of all the incredible people in the Bible who felt like they were not qualified to do the work that God had them do. For example, Esther was a young Jewish girl who was raised to the position of queen of a nation.

But more than that, God used her to save His people. Her enemy Haman certainly underestimated her. God's power and might were shown through the weakness of a young Jewish girl who was willing to lay everything down to do what was right.

Similarly, we often don't feel qualified to do the things that God has called us to do. When other people notice, we sometimes wonder why we thought we were able to serve God in that way in the first place.

But that's not how God sees us.

'NOLE NATION

Psalm 27:6 says, "And now my head shall be lifted up above my enemies all around me, and I will offer in his tent sacrifices with shouts of joy" (ESV). God doesn't leave us to be defeated, and our response needs to be that of joyful praise. Here are five ways we can allow ourselves to be used for God's glory, even when we don't feel qualified.

1. Don't argue when God calls you! He already knows what you think about your weakness. It's through our weakness that His glory shines.

2. Be prepared to be uncomfortable. God's plans often stretch us out of our comfort zones.

3. Watch for who God has called to be your helper. In scripture, we see time and time again that God provides a support system: Ruth for Naomi, Aaron for Moses, and Mordecai for Esther.

4. Wait for the opportune moment. Ask God for discernment and wisdom, and then listen for the prompting of the Holy Spirit.

5. Step out in faith. When God says to go, we have to go, even if we're nervous, scared, or can't see beyond the next step ahead.

Hebrews 11:1 tells us that faith is being sure of what we hope for. We don't know the given outcome or how God is going to work all things together for good (see Romans 8:28), but we know that He promises to do so. We simply have to play our part in His all-knowing plan, even when we can't see the next steps.

DAY 30
A SHOWDOWN BECOMES A LETDOWN

September 17, 2016: Louisville 63, Florida State 20
By Andy Clapp

For all have sinned and fall short of the glory of God.
—Romans 3:23 ESV

An early-season showcase turned into a Seminole disaster. Second-ranked Florida State traveled north to Louisville, hoping to handle a Top 10 obstacle early in the season. But it was the Cardinals who sped out of the gate to take an early lead.

Louisville hurried down the field and ended their first drive with a Lamar Jackson touchdown run from 2 yards out. Two minutes and six seconds into the game, Louisville led 7-0. Eight minutes later, Jackson ran the ball in from 14 yards out. 'Noles fans were stunned. Louisville threatened to eliminate the Seminoles in the first quarter of the game.

But Ricky Aguayo kicked a field goal from 47 yards out in the last two minutes of the first quarter. Then, early in the second quarter, Deondre Francois hit Auden Tate for a twenty-yard touchdown pass, pulling the 'Noles to within four, 14-10.

The Cardinals asserted their own will from that moment. Jeremy Smith ran for a touchdown, Lamar Jackson threw a touchdown to Jaylen Smith, and with twelve seconds left in the half, Jackson ran for his third rushing touchdown of the first half. When halftime arrived, the 'Noles faced a 35-10 deficit.

The Cardinals tacked on another four touchdowns in the second half. Lamar Jackson ran for his fourth rushing touchdown in the fourth quarter. The 'Noles managed 10 late points, but the game's outcome was decided by halftime. Louisville's quarterback accounted for five touchdowns.

What was hyped as a huge showdown turned into a colossal letdown for the 'Noles.

> For you are saved by grace through faith, and this is not from yourselves; it is God's gift—not from works, so that no one can boast. —Ephesians 2:8–9 HCSB

FEAR THE SPEAR

The project at work turned into a disaster, the outcome far removed from the outline of its origination. You reacted wrong to a situation at home and said some things that can never be taken back, words you wish you hadn't said. You burned supper or maybe forgot to pick up the dry cleaning. Today featured a fall. Some of our shortcomings can be easily dismissed, and some are colossal collapses. Some are overlooked by almost everyone, while others appear to be witnessed by the whole world. Falls and mistakes are a part of life.

'NOLE NATION

People fall flat on their faces in life. The 'Noles went to Louisville, and little to nothing went right. No one in the garnet and gold imagined the outcome when they boarded the plane in Florida to travel to Kentucky. The loss on a national stage stood as an embarrassment to a program that prided itself on excellence. When we step back, though, we see that every program has a bad day.

Paul talked about the one thing that every human has in common. We have many differences, whether it be our age, race, career choice, or personality. But in the middle of all the differences, there is one commonality. We've all blown it at some point in life. Paul wrote that every single one of us has sinned. Not one of us is perfect by a long shot.

The apostle taught that we all fall short in our quest for holiness and righteousness. But even in that reality, as we see our sinfulness and the penalty for those sins, the Lord offers us a do-over in life. He offers us the great restart of life with an opportunity to be born again in Jesus Christ.

You fell. There may be desperation as you look at how far you fell. Perhaps there is humiliation and embarrassment in the wake of the fall you've experienced. The realization sets in that our record before the Lord is no longer unblemished after we fall. But as long as there is breath in our lungs, we have the opportunity to stand before the Lord with a clean slate. (See 1 John 1:9)

So, how can such a fall turn into a new way of life? Here are a few points to ponder after a fall:

1. Embrace the humility—A fall leads us to a place of humbleness. When we realize our imperfections, we become more empathetic to those around us who have fallen in their lives.

2. Embrace grace—We are saved by grace, not by our works. Embrace the grace that God extends to you and value that grace.

Del Duduit, Andy Clapp, and Bethany Jett

3. Let go of shame—So often, we ask for forgiveness after we fall, but then we carry the shame of the fall long after we have turned the mistake over to the Lord. When Jesus took our sins to the cross, He took the guilt and the shame.

4. Ask the Lord to restore—The Lord is in the restoration business. He can put your life back together, and from that comes a testimony to His greatness.

5. Get back to kingdom work—Just as the season did not end after a 'Noles loss to Louisville, your life didn't end with a mistake. The Lord has you here for a purpose.

The 'Noles faced ridicule and humiliation after the fall at Louisville. The game left a mark on each player and coach, but their story wasn't over when the clock struck 0:00 in Louisville. Your story is not over either.

DAY 31
FEELS LIKE HOME

FSU Culture: Wescott Fountain
By Bethany Jett

Remember not the former things, nor consider the things of old. Behold, I am doing a new thing; now it springs forth, do you not perceive it? I will make a way in the wilderness and rivers in the desert. —Isaiah 43:18–19 ESV

Rumor has it that you're not officially a Florida State student until you've been tossed into the Wescott Fountain, and tradition holds that a Wescott Fountain dunking on your twenty-first birthday is in order. Additionally, Wescott Fountain is sometimes the unofficial eighteenth hole of impromptu games of disc golf.

Another Wescott Fountain tradition is the annual ring ceremony. To commemorate the foundation year of FSU—1851—each graduating senior dips his or her class ring into the fountain at exactly 18:51, or 6:51 p.m.

This beautiful fountain was a gift from the Florida State College for Women classes of 1915 and 1917 and is truly an homage to students of years past. From looking at the picturesque scene in front of Wescott Plaza, you would never know that it was once referred to as Gallows Hill, a place where many executions took place.

The fountain you see today is not the original. The original support structure completely failed in 1988, and the fountain was replaced by an exact replica. The fountain is surrounded by Brick Plaza, with each brick commemorating a special event, accomplishment, or person.

My favorite Wescott memory was when my eighteenth birthday was christened with an after-dinner toss into the fountain's waters. It may not have been my twenty-first birthday, as tradition holds, but the experience holds a special place in my heart, as it does with all students who get to call FSU home.

> So, [Pilate] delivered him over to them to be crucified. So they took Jesus, and he went out, bearing his own cross, to the place called The Place of a Skull, which in Aramaic is called Golgotha. —John 19:16–17 ESV

FEAR THE SPEAR

The haunting history of the Wescott Fountain's location being the spot of executions reminds one of another hill that was the spot of the most famous execution in the world. Although the bridge of the nose has eroded over time, Golgotha, or Calvary (Latin), is named for its resemblance to a skull.

Calvary is where our Savior took His last breath before dying on the cross for our sins. But, as we know, that breath was not His last, for He rose on the third day.

Likewise, we were, at one time, living vessels condemned to Hell because of our sins. But because of His great love for us, we are redeemed by the blood of Jesus that spilled on that hill, and today, we look forward to an eternity with Him.

'NOLE NATION

Have you ever tried really hard to make a big change in your life but felt yourself slipping back into old habits? The Bible says that we should not remember the former things because He is doing a new one. Just like a beautiful monument was constructed on a site where death had been prevalent, we are new creations in Christ—a soul that is alive instead of dead. So, here are five ways to let go of our old selves:

1. Give yourself grace. Jesus's blood washed away our sins. We are forgiven for eternity by our Savior, so it's time to cut ourselves some slack so we can let go of regret (see 1 John 1:9).

2. Forgive others. The Bible says that if we don't forgive others, God won't forgive us (see Matthew 6:14–15).

3. Change your habits. Is there anything that triggers a response to return to your old ways? Replace it quickly so that you can avoid the temptation altogether.

4. Transform. How can you redeem your past? Are there others who are struggling with a similar situation that you were once in? How can you give back?

5. Stay grounded in God's Word. Don't let busyness distract you from spending time with God every single day.

The blood of Jesus has washed away the stain of sin, and today, we are new creations with the purpose of helping others come to know our Savior. Don't ever let someone pull you back to where you were before.

DAY 32
SHINE ON, PRIME TIME

October 19, 1985: Florida State 76, Tulsa 14
By Andy Clapp

In the same way, let your light shine before men, so
that they may see your good works and give glory to
your Father in heaven. —Matthew 5:16 HCSB

Tulsa entered Doak Campbell hoping to shine in the Sunshine
State. But a freshman from FSU stole the show. His nickname,
"Prime Time," speaks to the very core of why FSU fans adored
him during his time in Tallahassee.

Tulsa started well, marching into 'Noles territory and
threatening to grab an early lead on the road. FSU, coming off
a blowout loss to Auburn, needed positive momentum. The
Seminole defense forced a fumble, which Tulsa recovered, but
the lost yards put the brakes on Tulsa's opening drive.

FSU moved down the field, their ground game imposing its
will on the Tulsa defense. An apparent touchdown was wiped off
the scoreboard because of a 'Noles penalty, but a field goal gave
the home crowd something to cheer for in the early moments.

After the defense recorded two sacks, Deion Sanders
dropped back to receive a punt. The freshman fielded the punt
and took it 34 yards, giving the offense possession deep in Tulsa
territory. Eric Thomas dropped back and hit Pat Carter for the
'Noles' first touchdown, pushing their lead to 10-0. After the

135

defense provided the team with an interception, Victor Floyd carried the ball in for another FSU touchdown.

Tulsa responded with a touchdown to pull within 10 points at 17-7, but that was the closest the visitors would draw the rest of the way.

The 'Noles scored a field goal and another Sanders punt return—37 yards this time—set up a Tony Smith rushing touchdown.

The Seminoles continued to dominate. Trailing 69-7, Tulsa drove to get into position for another score, hoping to make a moment to build on for the next game. Steve Gage threw into the end zone, but Sanders snagged the interception and returned the pick 100 yards for a touchdown. A perfect ending for the guy people knew as Prime Time.

> Whatever you do, do it enthusiastically, as something done for the Lord and not for men, knowing that you will receive the reward of an inheritance from the Lord.
> —Colossians 3:23–24 HCSB

FEAR THE SPEAR

As you head out the door today, flip the On switch for your life. What you do is needed and is necessary. Do it well and let the world see the potential in you. Think of it as a reflection of God's goodness. Stand out in the crowd rather than blending in with the bland. Your life is called to shine in the darkest of times. You may feel the stage is too big for you, but it's not too big for God. You may feel a bit underequipped for the moment, but use what the Lord has given you, and He will bless it.

'NOLE NATION

We hold back too much. We fear the stage but need to face all of life with faith. God's people are created to triumph. We are called to stand out from everyone else in this world, not because we are great but because the Lord is great!

Jesus stood before a multitude gathered on a hillside early in His ministry. The people longed for definition in life. And the Author of life taught them what true life looks like. He gave meaning and purpose. After Jesus talked about those He called blessed, He spoke words that inspire all of us to live life out loud.

He called His listeners—ordinary men and women—the light of the world. Most felt common, but He called them to an extraordinary life. Jesus told them to let their light shine before men. By living out loud, excelling every day as the light of the world shines through them, they brought glory to their Father in heaven.

For you and me, it may not be 100-yard interception returns before fifty-thousand onlookers, but it is the good works God has equipped us to do. As we carry out what God calls us to do, we shine a light in the world. Jesus told them to turn it on and point to the Father as they took the field of life each day. So how do we keep our light shining every day? Here are a few ideas to consider:

1. Stand out—Life can blend in, or it can stand out. Live a radiant life by reflecting the light of Christ in all that you say and do. How we stand out is simply by living differently. When we live like Christ, the world will take notice.

2. Don't fear the stage—We need to stand out so that others may come to know Jesus through our lives. The task may seem huge, but doing the simple things well will lead to the right results.

3. Believe in yourself and believe in God—Trust the timing in life. As God has instilled in you the ability to do certain things, He has also put you in a position to use those abilities to bring glory to His name.

4. Don't sit on the sidelines—Many are happy to ride the sidelines in life. Get in the game. Showcase what you can do and refuse to sit back idle, failing to use what the Lord has given to you.

5. Give it all you've got—Step up and go all out. Don't hold back one ounce.

Deion Sanders lived up to his nickname throughout his college and professional careers. He remains as one of the players never to be forgotten. The lights are shining, and we need to be the ones who showcase the talents we have. We need others to see how big our God is and how He can perform the incredible in our lives.

DAY 33
SUPPORT ONE ANOTHER

September 20, 2014: Florida State 23, Clemson 16
By Del Duduit

But as for you, O man of God, flee these things. Pursue righteousness, godliness, faith, love, steadfastness, gentleness. —1 Timothy 6:11 ESV

A lot was riding on the game.

Florida State's 18-game winning streak was on the line. The Seminoles' starting quarterback, Jameis Winston, had been suspended, and the backup QB, Sean Maguire, had never started a game. And the ACC opener was with rival Clemson.

A mighty big mountain was in front of 'Nole Nation.

Sean Maguire was nervous but ready to make his debut under center. Maguire, a redshirt sophomore, completed just six of his first 17 attempts in the first half and was chased around and knocked down by the Clemson defense.

But in the third quarter, Maguire led his team downfield for a 68-yard drive that culminated with a Mario Pender 1-yard plunge to tie the game, 10-10.

After Clemson scored a TD, Maguire again responded well under pressure. He fired a 74-yard touchdown pass to Rashad Greene to tie the game 17-17 in the fourth.

The Tiger defense picked off a Maguire pass with a couple of minutes left in the game and marched down into Seminole territory. Then 'Noles defensive tackle C. J. Davidson stripped the ball from a Clemson running back to preserve the tie and send the game into overtime.

The Seminole defense stuffed the Tigers on their first possession to set the stage for Maguire and the offense. Two plays later, running back Karlos Williams dashed into the end zone from 13 yards out to give FSU a thrilling 23-17 win.

After the game, Maguire attributed his performance to his teammate Winston, who had to watch the game from the sideline. Maguire told reporters that the two stayed up late at night watching film together and preparing for the game.

"He was telling me what he was seeing; I was telling him what I was seeing. He was awesome," Maguire said.

Maguire called Winston his biggest supporter and cheerleader.

Iron sharpens iron, and one man sharpens another.
—Proverbs 27:17 ESV

How do you support your friends in tough times?

FEAR THE SPEAR

Do you have a friend who is facing a difficult situation? Have you reached out to be a friend, or have you chosen not to be involved? What would you do if a friend was accused of something they did not do? Would you come to his side? Would you have his back? Would you take the heat for your association with them? What if your friend's reputation is put to the task and his character is under scrutiny?

'NOLE NATION

It's easy to sit back and watch, but it takes courage to help a brother in need. Taking a stand sometimes means losing friends or coming under fire for your associations. Would you help a friend in a tough time? Here are some ways you can be a true friend who can be counted on when the chips are down.

1. Pray for them: Don't just go through the motions—really pray for them. Take the extra time each day to lift them up to your heavenly Father. Be specific and ask the Lord for guidance and discernment. There is no better way to support a friend in need than to spend valuable time on your knees in prayer. "And above all these put on love, which binds everything together in perfect harmony" (Colossians 3:14 ESV).

2. Be an encourager: A simple text or a call to tell a friend you are thinking about him can do wonders. It could mean the world to them if you offer to run an errand or stop by with some dinner. Make sure your friends know you are available to talk or chat, and this might be just what they need to encourage them to keep going. "Therefore encourage one another and build one another up, just as you are doing" (1 Thessalonians 5:11 ESV).

3. Spend time with them: Your time is the most valuable commodity you have. And when you can carve out a few minutes to spend with a friend who is down, it can lift their spirits high. Meet for a coffee or invite them for a round of golf. Find a way to let him know you care.

Del Duduit, Andy Clapp, and Bethany Jett

4. Try to understand their perspective: Even if you disagree with your friend, give them the benefit of the doubt. Stop and consider his viewpoint as unique and respect his opinion. You don't have to agree with or endorse his way of thinking, but you should strive to understand where he is coming from and what has influenced his decisions. You and your friend should be able to have a mature conversation about your differences and not feel like it is your duty to change each other's minds.

5. Show comfort: Be a beacon of support and comfort to your friends when they are going through a tough time. Try to walk in their shoes so you can relate to their problems. Pray together with them that God will comfort them in their time of need and wrap His arms around them and give them peace. They might even just need a good hug to soothe their weary souls. "The LORD is near to the brokenhearted and saves the crushed in spirit" (Psalm 34:18 ESV).

Winston knew he could not play, but he did all he could to support Maguire in his backup role to lead him to success as the starter. The two spent hours in preparation and consulted regularly during the game. Maguire counted on Winston's experience to help him win the game. You can also be an encourager and a friend to help lead others to a life of victory.

DAY 34
FROM TRAGEDY TO TRIUMPH

November 16, 1996: Florida State 54, Southern Mississippi 14
By Andy Clapp

We know that all things work together for the good of
those who love God: those who are called according to
His purpose. —Romans 8:28 HCSB

The Seminoles faced off against the Southern Miss Golden
Eagles as the 1996 season drew to a close.

Thad Busby, coming off an injury, sailed his first pass of the
game. Southern Miss took advantage, returning the interception inside the red zone. Within the first two minutes of the
game, the 'Noles faced a 7-0 deficit.

The Golden Eagles led, but their momentum was short-
lived.

Four minutes later, Florida State responded. Star running
back Warrick Dunn scored his first touchdown of the game.
Before the quarter ended, Busby atoned for his early interception with an 8-yard strike to Laveranues Coles to put the home
team ahead 14-7.

Southern Miss pulled even early in the second quarter,
squaring the score at 14-14. However, the Seminoles throttled the Eagles from that point forward. Busby went 4-4 on a
drive that ended with a Rock Preston touchdown. Though the
offense committed two turnovers after gaining the lead, the

defense stiffened and even forced a safety to put the Seminoles ahead, 23-14.

Warrick Dunn added a fifteen-yard touchdown run in the third quarter, as well as a 77-yard touchdown reception. Thad Busby hit Dunn on a screen pass, and he bolted 77 yards down the field for a touchdown. Dunn's electric play reminded the world why he was one of the greatest to play college football. The touchdown also gave Warrick Dunn the all-time record for touchdowns scored at Florida State.

Dan Kendra relieved Thad Busby and kept the offense rolling down the field. Kendra hit Coles and Ron Dugans for touchdowns in the fourth quarter, nailing the door shut on any hope the Eagles had for victory.

> But thanks be to God, who gives us the victory through our Lord Jesus Christ! —1 Corinthians 15:57 HCSB

FEAR THE SPEAR

Life knows tragedies. No one avoids at least one tragedy in their life. For some, it is the unplanned sickness that alters what will be for a season or possibly forever. An act of evil takes away someone of critical importance in our lives. At the point of the tragedy, questions arise about how to move forward in a new reality. New responsibilities mark new realities brought on by a tragic occurrence. Pain lingers in the aftermath, not only for a month but for the rest of someone's life. Can triumph be experienced after a tragedy strikes? Is there hope that propels us when hopelessness seems to dominate our days?

'NOLE NATION

Warrick Dunn raced into the Florida State history books with another touchdown, the triumph of any athlete. What made the story even more inspiring was his ability to turn tragedy into triumph. Dunn's mother, Betty Smothers, an off-duty police officer, had been killed in an ambush while Warrick was in high school. In that one moment, his plans and his responsibilities changed. But the rest of his story reveals how triumph can emerge from trauma.

Paul wrote to the believers in Rome, assuring them that the Lord has a plan. He spoke of the groans of life but assured that those groans would give way to glory one day. To further strengthen those who faced tragedies, Paul revealed that all things come together for good for those who believe. Did it mean that nothing bad would happen to believers? No. But it did teach that God can take the worst of what happens in our lives and creates something positive.

Tragedies threaten to thwart the life God has planned for us. The unimaginable can hold power enough to shatter our dreams, but God holds the ultimate power. His ability to rewrite the story of our lives has been witnessed since the beginning of time. And along the way, He has taken tragedies and turmoil, the beginning points of one's story, and produced triumphs that are trumpeted unto today.

Lazarus died, but his story didn't end there. The groaning and grieving of his sisters turned to the glory of the Lord with a few words from Jesus. Likewise, Mephibosheth was thought to be as good as dead after becoming lame until he was invited to sit at the king's table. These are just a few examples.

Del Duduit, Andy Clapp, and Bethany Jett

How can we overcome the tragedy to experience triumph? Here are some things to consider:

1. Remember God—We are quick to blame the Lord in moments of tragedy. But remember stories like Mephibosheth, Lazarus, and countless others. Turn to His word and see how He can turn the story around.

2. Be reminded of truth—We believe that there is always more time. Let tragedy be a reminder that time is limited on this earth.

3. Reflect and react—How can someone else's life be altered in the wake of a tragedy? Look for ways God can use this event to save the life of another person.

4. Remember that you are not alone—Paul talks earlier in Romans 8 about the Spirit's involvement when we are so broken that we can only groan. Even in the grief, we are not alone. The Lord has not abandoned you.

5. Press forward—Though it may take some time, you have a purpose, and God still has a plan.

Warrick Dunn's story inspires us. He faced an unspeakable tragedy at an early age. But resiliency won the day and a life marred by tragedy became a life marked by triumph. So many people were touched by his story and his success, and as a result, lives were changed.

DAY 35
BE WARY OF YOUR OPPONENT

January 6, 2014: FSU 34, Auburn 31
By Bethany Jett

Be sober-minded; be watchful. Your adversary the devil prowls around like a roaring lion, seeking someone to devour. Resist him, firm in your faith, knowing that the same kinds of suffering are being experienced by your brotherhood throughout the world.
—1 Peter 5:8–9 ESV

The 2013 regular season ended with freshman Jameis Winston's name on the lips of everyone impressed with the young FSU quarterback from Alabama. Finally, Florida State was ready to win another national championship, and their opponent, also hailing from Alabama, was a force to be reckoned with.

Auburn University was the favorite, with a series of miracle plays leading them to compete with FSU for the title. In fact, Auburn was dubbed the "team of destiny" after the football bounced off two Georgia Bulldog players into the hands of Auburn for a touchdown to win a game, and then again after Auburn's Kick Six, where they caught the ball in the end zone with one second left and ran it for a touchdown to win. Auburn won the SEC title the following week and was now poised to play Florida State.

The first three quarters of the game did not go the way Florida State wanted. Auburn led going into the final quarter, and it seemed that perhaps destiny truly was on Auburn's side. But the 'Noles rallied and pulled the score to 31-27. All the 'Noles needed was a touchdown to secure their victory.

Winston completed a 49-yard pass to Rashad Greene to the Auburn two-yard line. With seconds left, Winston threw the much-needed last touchdown pass to Kelvin Benjamin to secure the win.

The talent on Florida State's field during the 2013 season led to a record number of most draft picks in a three-year window, a Heisman for Winston, and NFL careers for several of the players.

Rumor has it that Auburn knew the FSU play calls. Whether it was because Auburn's new co-offensive coordinator Dameyune Craig had spent the last three seasons coaching under Head Coach Jimbo Fisher at Florida State, or because Auburn had time to break down the patterns of the offensive plays, the Seminoles held up towels to cover the coaches so the plays couldn't be seen.[6]

Once the play calls were no longer visible, FSU rallied, with the Florida State offense increasing their yards-per-play by about 75 percent.[7] In a press conference, Fisher said, "[Auburn] had a couple of our signals a couple times and were getting to them. That happens, people do it, and that's our fault. You've

---

[6] Jason Staples, "How Did Auburn Steal FSU's Signals?" 247Sports.com, January 26, 2014, https://247sports.com/college/florida-state/Article/How-Did-Auburn-Steal-FSUs-Signals-105069253/.

[7] Staples, "How Did Auburn Steal FSU's Signals?"

got to change them, constantly rotate them. . . . That's part of the game."[8]

> Put on the whole armor of God, that you may be able to stand against the schemes of the devil. For we do not wrestle against flesh and blood, but against the rulers, against the authorities, against the cosmic powers over this present darkness, against the spiritual forces of evil in the heavenly places. —Ephesians 6:11–12 ESV

FEAR THE SPEAR

Just like Jimbo Fisher wasn't surprised that the Auburn team may have known their play calls, we should not be surprised that we have an enemy who is always watching for ways to interfere. But, once the Florida State coaches realized what was happening, they pivoted. They moved.

Likewise, when we realize a spiritual attack is happening, we must also make a change. But unlike the coaches on the sidelines of the game, we don't have to hide behind towels to have conversations with our heavenly Father. Our armor is a spiritual one. It doesn't matter if the devil is listening or not because he has no power where our God is concerned.

'NOLE NATION

The scripture warns us to be watchful for the devil's tricks. Here are five ways we can protect ourselves from the enemy:

---

[8] Joel A. Erickson, "Florida State's Jimbo Fisher Says Auburn 'Had a Couple of Our Signals,'" Alabama.com, January 7, 2014, https://www.al.com/auburnfootball/2014/01/florida_states_jimbo_fisher_sa.html.

1. Understand who is in control. We have no power against the enemy. It is God's power, not ours. Even the archangel Michael did not take on Satan by himself. He called on the power of Jesus.

2. Learn to identify a spiritual attack by staying rooted in scripture. Did you know that the best way to identify a counterfeit is not to study the forgeries but the original? It doesn't matter what the fakes look like as long as you know what to look for in the genuine piece. Similarly, the best way to know when something is not of God is to know what *is* of God.

3. Bathe yourself in prayer. We have a direct connection with God and can pray continuously, without ceasing. And when we don't know what to pray, the Holy Spirit prays on our behalf (see Romans 8:26).

4. Memorize the Word of God. The enemy is deceitful. In the garden of Eden and with Jesus in the desert, the devil twisted God's words around. We have to know what scripture says so we'll know the lies when we hear them.

5. Call on Jesus. John 14:3 says, "Whatever you ask in my name, this I will do, that the Father may be glorified in the Son." We are confident that by the name of Jesus, all creation must bow down to Him, and that includes Satan himself.

Remember: Fight the good fight and when you're going through an attack from the enemy, remember God's promise in 1 Peter

5:10: "And after you have suffered a little while, the God of all grace, who has called you to his eternal glory in Christ, will himself restore, confirm, strengthen, and establish you."

DAY 36
BE THE DEFENDER

October 5, 1968: Florida State 20, Texas A&M 14
By Andy Clapp

Don't be afraid of them. Remember the great and awe-inspiring Lord, and fight for your countrymen, your sons and daughters, your wives and homes.
—Nehemiah 4:14 HCSB

After a disappointing 9-3 loss to the Florida Gators, the Seminoles took the field, needing a win before their open date. The Aggies of Texas A&M also needed a victory to break the .500 mark for the season.

The defense of the Seminoles became the story of the game. FSU took the lead midway through the first quarter when Bill Cappleman hit Jim Tyson for a six-yard touchdown. The 'Noles offense produced more in the first quarter against the Aggies than in four quarters against the Gators.

But A&M fought back. Using the ground attack to enforce their will, the Aggies scored two rushing touchdowns in less than three minutes to wrangle a 14-7 lead.

Grant Guthrie hit a 27-yard field goal to pull the Seminoles within four. Then, with three minutes to go in the half, Cappleman threw another touchdown—a 14-yard strike to Billy Cox to give FSU a 17-14 halftime lead.

The only scoring in the second half was a Grant Guthrie 40-yard field goal in the fourth quarter, pushing the Seminole lead to six.

The Aggies refused to give in and drove the field in search of the winning touchdown. Threatening to steal a win, Edd Hargett dropped back, prepared to push his team to victory. But Walt Sumner picked off the pass with forty-six seconds to go, slamming the door on the comeback.

The FSU defense intercepted the Aggies four times in the game. Dale McCullers had a record-setting game with twenty-nine tackles, and the defense also recovered a fumble. The defense stepped up, shutting out the Aggies in the second half, delivering the victory the team needed so desperately.

> No one will be able to stand against you as long as you live. I will be with you, just as I was with Moses. I will not leave you or forsake you. —Joshua 1:5 HCSB

FEAR THE SPEAR

The enemy looks for a crack in your life and tries to gain a foothold. He knows that your attitude opens itself up to negativity, so he preys on your attitude. A coworker gets under your skin, so the enemy uses them in a direct attempt to derail your day. Earthly life threatens to infiltrate your spiritual life when the television swarms your mind with images. Greed takes root, enticing you to worship money above all else. With life, there comes temptation, but you have the choice to stand.

'NOLE NATION

The opponent threw all it had at the Seminoles that day, but the defense ensured that the Aggies went back to College Station with a loss. Dale McCullers served as a fortified wall. He plugged the gaps, saw where Texas A&M plotted to gain ground, and put a stop to their attack. With 29 tackles for the game, he ensured the 'Noles end zone stayed protected.

Nehemiah's heart broke at the news of the condition of Jerusalem. The city lay in ruins, and though Nehemiah had never been to Jerusalem, it was the home of his ancestors. One of the biggest issues was that the city's wall had been decimated. As a result, enemies could come and go as they wanted, leaving Jerusalem open to be pillaged at will.

He traveled to the city and organized the rebuild. Each group worked on specific sections, and Nehemiah issued a call to the builders and the defenders. He prepared them and implored them to be ready to defend against any attack. He also motivated them by teaching them to do it, to guard and fortify, for the sake of those around them—friends, family, and countrymen.

They say that football is a game of inches, but the game of life is one of centimeters. If you give the devil even a centimeter of space, he will try to establish a foothold and invade your entire life. Our goal is to win in life for the glory of God, and being solid in our defense against the enemy's attack is important not only for ourselves but also for those around us. So how do we build the wall of defense in our life? Here are some ideas to consider:

1. Commit to defense—Lackadaisical attitudes allow for unforeseen advances by the enemy. Develop the mindset that there is no room for the enemy in your life. Keep him at bay by committing to keep him out.

2. Build a wall—The Word of God is a mighty fortress. Those who long to keep the enemy out build up their defense by the Word of God.

3. Identify weak areas—Some areas of life are weaker than others. You may not struggle with lust, but gossip threatens to overtake your life and testimony. See those areas as a part of the wall that needs extra attention.

4. See the impact—A city wall protected all of its residents. So, everyone benefited from a well-established wall. The defense in your life will help not only you but those around you.

5. Don't give a millimeter—Keep up the resolve. Refuse to give even a millimeter.

The defense won the day when the Aggies and 'Noles squared off. Dale McCullers did his job and the whole team benefited from the one unwilling to give an inch. The 'Noles had a bye week to rest, and they rested more easily after the defense secured the victory over the Aggies.

DAY 37

THERE IS NOTHING LIKE CONFIDENCE

November 26, 1988: Florida State 52, Florida 17
By Del Duduit

Therefore, do not throw away your confidence, which
has a great reward. For you have need of endurance,
so that when you have done the will of God you may
receive what is promised. —Hebrews 10:35–36 ESV

Florida State was ranked No. 5 and plowed over visiting Florida
52-17 in front of a record crowd of about 62,700 fans at Doak
Campbell Stadium in Tallahassee on a crisp Saturday night.

The Seminoles scored on their first three possessions, and
the rout was on.

For the Gators, the loss would be the second-worst defeat
in history against the 'Noles. In 1977, FSU crushed the Gators,
37-9.

FSU quarterback Chip Ferguson threw for 131 yards and
completed 10 of 16 attempts. He tossed TD passes to Lawrence
Dawsey (18 yards), Tom O'Malley (15 yards), and Sammie
Smith (8 yards).

Defensive player Marion Butts recovered a Florida fumble
in the end zone for a TD, and Odell Haggins picked off a Gator
pass and returned it 8 yards for a pick-six.

The game was so bad for the Gators that running back
Emmitt Smith, who entered the game needing only 68 yards

to reach the 1,000-yard mark, finished with only 56 yards on 15 carries.

You may have noticed that one name did not appear in any of the previous highlights—Deion Sanders, who set the stage before the game started. The flashy and brilliant player showed up for the nationally televised game in style. He wanted everyone to know how confident he was in himself and his team. There was also a chance that a win could boost the Seminoles to the No.-1 ranking in college football and a possible Sugar Bowl bid.

In the final home game of his career, Sanders, a two-time unanimous All-American, pulled up to the locker room in a limousine. He stepped out dressed in a full black tuxedo to the delight of the massive and rowdy crowd.

Then he strolled into the locker room to prepare himself for the game.

This exciting moment gave his teammates the confidence they needed to go out and knock off the Gators.

Confidence is a wonderful trait to possess.

Have I not commanded you? Be strong and coura-
geous. Do not be frightened, and do not be dismayed,
for the LORD your God is with you wherever you go.
—Joshua 1:9 ESV

FEAR THE SPEAR

Has someone ever tried to bully you or make you feel inferior because you are a child of God? Has anyone tried to put you down because you don't follow the world? Maybe someone at school or on the job makes fun of you and belittles you because of your beliefs. Does that make you feel ashamed of the gospel?

'NOLE NATION

While you cannot control what others might say or think about you, you can keep it from impacting your self-confidence. After all, *you* are a child of the King of Kings. You are special and unique. There is a big difference between arrogance and confidence. The Lord does not like His children to be cocky, but He does want you to be confident in your salvation. There are many benefits to having a relationship with Christ, and here are some ways you can show your confidence in the Savior.

1. Obedience builds confidence: When you obey the Lord, you will be blessed beyond measure. This does not mean your life will be without problems, but you will have the freedom to overcome them with the help of the Holy Spirit. Trust God through your battles and look to Him for the answers. When Christ is in control of your life, you will be at peace. "Blessed is the man who trusts in the LORD, whose trust is the LORD. He is like a tree planted by water, that sends out its roots by the stream, and does not fear when heat comes, for its leaves remain green, and is not anxious in the year of drought, for it does not cease to bear fruit" (Jeremiah 17:7–8 ESV).

2. Prayer promotes confidence: A good conversation with your best friend or spouse is an investment in your relationship. Your prayers with the Master should also bring peace and comfort. God is always there when you need to pour your heart out to Him, and that's OK. But

don't forget to also take the chance to thank Him for being good to you.

3. Opportunities build confidence: If you pray and ask the Lord to open doors for you to help others, He will. But it's up to you to take advantage of these opportunities. Smile and say good morning to someone on an elevator. Tell a waitress what a great job he or she did and leave a gospel tract with a tip to let them know that Jesus loves them. You can pay for a stranger's cup of coffee or send a kind text to a friend you know is going through a hard time. There are multiple ways to show the love of Christ and build your confidence as a witness of his goodness.

4. Service strengthens confidence: It can be eye-opening when you give of your time and money to help someone in need. Serving food in a homeless shelter or wrapping Christmas presents for a toy drive will take dedicated time out of your day but assisting others who need it is fulfilling and will make you see just how blessed you really are. Show God's love and mercy by giving yourself to those who are less fortunate.

5. God wants you to be confident: He does not want you to live a defeated life. On the contrary, he wants the best for you. Will you have problems? Yes. Will you face tragedy? Maybe. But you can rest assured knowing God will win the game in the end. In the meantime, you can feel as if you are pulling up to His house in style. "The LORD will fulfill his purpose for me; your steadfast love, O LORD, endures forever. Do not forsake the work of your hands" (Psalm 138:8 ESV).

There Is Nothing Like Confidence

Give the Lord praise and honor—He is on your side. Knowing that your sins are forgiven, and you will have a home in heaven should give you all the confidence you need to live a glorious life for the kingdom.

DAY 38
THE BOWDEN LEGACY

January 12, 1976—January 1, 2010
By Bethany Jett

It was not you who sent me here, but God. —Genesis
45:8 ESV

"I care where my players spend eternity," Head Coach Bobby
Bowden said. "I've always tried to serve God's purpose for my
life, on and off the field."

Who knew that the eighth head coach in Florida State
football history would be the one to become iconic of what
being an FSU Seminole represents? Bobby Bowden created
a dynasty in the years he coached (1976–2009). Seminoles.
com says, "In addition, the win gave Bowden his 33rd straight
winning season and moved his career record to 389-129-4."

Coach Bowden's success, however, did not come without
setbacks. As a child, rheumatic fever wracked his body, and
doctors predicted he'd never play sports again, let alone achieve
his dream of coaching at the University of Alabama.

Bowden joined the 'Noles in 1963 as the wide receiver
coach. Later after massive success at FSU, that childhood
dream came calling, but after realizing he wasn't the top choice,
Bowden turned around and headed back south to Tallahassee,
where he remained until his retirement.

Bowden's reputation as a head coach went beyond his win-loss record. He was a mentor to the young men who came through his program. It's said that he could, and would, deal with anything except lying, a policy that allows for a lot of grace because trust is there at the foundation of the relationship. Cementing his faith and his role as leader, Bowden was known to take the team to church twice a year and constantly quote scripture.

But Bowden did more than just talk about the Bible; he lived it out. Bowden was a man of his word. His yes was yes, and his no was no. So, when Chris Weinke initially declined to come to FSU to play football, instead choosing to pursue baseball, Coach Bowden told him he'd still have a spot if he changed his mind. Fast forward and Bowden is about to recruit a hotshot quarterback when lo and behold, he gets a call from Weinke.

Bowden kept his word and brought Weinke on, a decision which led to Weinke winning the Heisman and leading the Seminoles to a national championship title in 1999.

> Blessed is the one who perseveres under trial because, having stood the test, that person will receive the crown of life that that Lord has promised to those who love him. —James 1:12 NIV

FEAR THE SPEAR

Bobby Bowden often joked that the ACLU would come after him for living out his bold faith on and off the field. Here was a man, larger than life, with press and cameras constantly following him around, who was unafraid of repercussions.

Faith was greater than fear.

It could be said that Coach Bowden was destined for Florida State football to lead the teams to national championships and create a legacy for the school. But I believe God brought him to Tallahassee to mentor young men, be a godly role model in their lives, and lead by example.

We see in scripture how God uses people to fulfill His purpose, and while many believe that He favors the garnet and gold, the truth is that God places us in situations so that His glory shines through.

Take Joseph in the book of Genesis. His jealous brothers sold him into slavery, where he was later imprisoned before taking up a high position in Egypt. When his brothers are distressed for their part, Joseph says, "You did not send me here, but God."

But God.

Where is God calling you? Where has He sent you?

God was fulfilling a promise to Abraham through Joseph, for indeed, it is because of Joseph's position that they were able to be saved.

'NOLE NATION

When God calls us, we have to be ready, no matter how big the opposition. No matter how many people are watching.

Here are five ways to make sure we're listening to God's voice.

1. Quiet your spirit before God. Give Him a chance to speak to you. The Bible says that "Whoever is of God hears the words of God. The reason why you do not hear them is that you are not of God" (John 8:47 ESV). If

you're having trouble hearing from God, quiet yourself, ask God to search your heart and reveal any areas of sin that you need to deal with. Tell Him that you're anxious to hear from Him. And then wait.

2. Listen. We have to maintain our relationship with God so we can hear His voice. Just like sheep know their shepherd's voice, we have to learn to listen to God. This is done through our prayer time, reading the scripture, and meditating on God's word.

3. Surround yourself with other believers. Listen to their counsel. Sometimes God uses other Christians to help provide us with direction.

4. Be ready to go when God calls you. Put the details in place so you're ready when God says it's time to go.

5. Act. It's OK to be unsure about what the next step is, but sometimes we must step out in faith. God doesn't always show us the full path forward, and to be honest, if He did, we might be too afraid to walk down that path.

In all things, we strive to bring God glory. We don't know always know *why* God calls us to certain places, but we know that we can serve Him faithfully while we are there. Just like we can look at the men and women of Bible days and learn from their example, we too can take an example from Coach Bobby Bowden's playbook.

In memory of our greatest head coach, glory be to God, and hail FSU.

DAY 39

IT'S A NEW DAY, NO MATTER WHAT THEY SAY

November 13, 1999: Florida State 49, Maryland 10
By Andy Clapp

As far as the east is from the west, so far has He removed our transgressions from us. —Psalm 103:12 HCSB

Everyone everywhere had an opinion.

As the 'Noles continued their quest to a second national championship, issues off the field created more chatter than did the play on the field. One of the central figures was star receiver Peter Warrick, who faced shoplifting charges from a department store and sat out a couple of games for a suspension.

Newspapers ran columns. Analysts commented on the situation, many saying he should be kicked off the team. Later in the season, Gators fans chanted and held up bags from the store to taunt the best player in football.

After struggling in his first game back, Warrick took the field against the Terps with a new mindset. FSU—ranked No. 1—looked unbeatable for the first in quite some time.

Ron Dugans caught a six-yard pass to start the scoring. After Maryland kicked a field goal, Peter Warrick took control. Quarterback Chris Weinke hit Warrick for another touchdown.

Dugans, not to be outdone, scored his second touchdown of the game three minutes later, putting the Seminoles up 21-3. Atrews Bell hauled in a 30-yard touchdown pass from the red-hot Weinke in the last minute of the first half.

Cruising with a 28-3 lead in the third quarter, the stars could have eased up. They didn't. There were voices to be silenced. Warrick hauled in two touchdown passes in the third quarter. His scores put the 'Noles up 42-3, slamming the door on the Terps.

Warrick caught nine passes for 134 yards and three touchdowns. He shut out the noise surrounding him to take care of the business ahead of him on the field.

> For am I now trying to win the favor of people, or God? Or am I striving to please people? If I were still trying to please people, I would not be a slave of Christ.
> —Galatians 1:10 HCSB

FEAR THE SPEAR

You hear the negativity. Voices rise in a chorus of accusations of what you did wrong. Even when you think it's behind you, whispers continue. What makes it even worse is when we hear the enemy taunting us for the mistakes we have made. The scowls of others and the antagonization of the enemy cause us to replay our mistakes over and over. The pain of the situation causes you to wonder if you can ever move past your past or if the rest of your days will feature a soundtrack of unchangeable sorrows.

'NOLE NATION

There will always be those who talk about who you were. Every mistake you made ends up in a conversation. The devil spends every single minute reminding you of your failings. The more we listen, the more frozen we become.

Zacchaeus overcame the hatred of man. His tax collecting days had accumulated much wealth for him and racked up many enemies. Yet Jesus called him to come down from the tree. Jesus drew the diminutive man to Himself so he could live a new life, regardless of what anyone else thought of that call. If he had listened to the people, he never would have reached out to new life. But he let the past be the past as he took the step of faith to move forward.

The Bible says that when we confess our sins to the Lord, those mistakes are removed from us as far as the east is from the west. When the Lord looks at you, He is not looking down on you due to your past. Christ died on the cross to deal with our past so we can embark on a new future.

The enemy is the father of accusations. He longs to derail you every day of the rest of your life by highlighting every bad moment. He points out every terrible action, every regretful word, and in doing so, tries to keep you shackled to what Christ set you free from. So many live under a weight that Jesus has already lifted. Don't listen to those lies from Satan. Take the field today remembering that Jesus took care of what we couldn't fix on our own.

Here are some truths to remember when Satan says you will never overcome who you were:

1. Only one opinion matters—Paul understood this truth better than most. He wrote Galatians 1:10—that verse

alone gives us the perspective we need to break free from the shackles of man's opinions.

2. You are forgiven—the Lord cannot lie. As John proclaimed in 1 John 1:9, you are forgiven when you confess your sins. When the enemy accuses, remind him that you are forgiven.

3. Don't look back—Paul wrote that he forgets what was and presses on to what is and what will be. Looking back never propels people forward. Looking back only locks you in an unchangeable past.

4. Let the persecution lead to praise—when you hear of your mistakes, praise the Lord that He changed your life. Who you were is not who you are now—praise Him for doing such a great work.

5. Keep on keeping on—if the Lord didn't want to use you anymore, He could have banished you. You are here. He is here. And He can use you.

Peter Warrick messed up. His mistake cost him the Heisman Trophy, but he overcame all the negative voices and opinions to lead his team to a national championship. The chants were loud. The heckling followed him for some time. But he kept going, and his play spoke volumes as he moved on in his life.

DAY 40
TOUGH LOVE

November 4, 2000: Florida State 54, Clemson 7
By Del Duduit

Love is patient and kind; love does not envy or boast;
it is not arrogant or rude. It does not insist on its own
way; it is not irritable or resentful; it does not rejoice
at wrongdoing but rejoices with the truth. Love bears
all things, believes all things, hopes all things, endures
all things. Love never ends. As for prophecies, they will
pass away; as for tongues, they will cease; as for knowledge, it will pass away. —1 Corinthians 13:4–8 ESV

The Florida State offense rolled over conference rival Clemson
with a whopping 771 yards and thrashed the Tigers 54-7 at
Doak Campbell Stadium in Tallahassee, Florida.

Seminoles quarterback Chris Weinke passed for 521 yards
in the win. He also set a record in the first quarter when he
used a play-action fake, stood with his back to the defense in
the end zone, turned, and fired a bullet to a wide-open Snoop
Minnis, who took it to the house for a 98-yard TD.

That was a sign of things to come.

Florida State Head Coach Bobby Bowden poured it on and
sent a message to No. 4-ranked Clemson's head coach—his son
Tommy Bowden.

Papa Bowden said after the game that he felt bad after his team thumped his boy's squad by 47 points. But he added that his son needed to go through similar things he experienced as a young head coach.

Maybe Papa Bowden poured it on a little too much when FSU backup Davy Ford ran 82-yards for a touchdown toward the end of the game.

The younger Bowden kneeled on the sideline and put his head in his hands while the Seminole faithful chanted "Who's your daddy?" several times.

For each will have to bear his own load.
—Galatians 6:5 ESV

Tough love.

Have you had to show it to a loved one? Have you been on the receiving end? How did it make you feel? Did you learn from it?

FEAR THE SPEAR

What is tough love? It's the willingness to do *tough* things with the right intentions and with love. Most of the time, it's done to teach a lesson or demonstrate discipline. It's the refusal to enable or reward negative or harmful behavior. Remember when Nathan confronted King David about his sin? After King David committed adultery and had his lover's husband killed in battle, Nathan spoke up to David and told him the truth. That was tough love. Maybe you have a friend who is going down the wrong path, and you feel you must say something to intervene before it's too late. Or perhaps you have to find a different crowd to hang out with when your current friends are making bad choices. You may even have to sit down with your spouse or child and confront them about their own mistakes.

'NOLE NATION

Showing tough love is not fun. But it has to be done when God instructs you or perhaps it's the last resort in a painful situation. Did your parents ever tell you, "This will hurt me more than it hurts you?" It's true. No parent enjoys discipline or showing tough love. But there are times when it is necessary. If you find yourself in this situation, make sure you show tough love for the right reasons.

1. Do not compromise your convictions: If you are a parent, your job is not to be your child's buddy. You might be the only one who tells them "No." And they may argue and whine, but they also appreciate your concern. Don't give in to pressure to be the "cool parent" or "cool friend." Integrity is a wonderful trait to show, and your children will be better adults when you teach them what is right. "For the moment all discipline seems painful rather than pleasant, but later it yields the peaceful fruit of righteousness to those who have been trained by it" (Hebrews 12:11 ESV).

2. Use it to witness to others: You can tell your friends that you don't want to go out to a wild party because you want to stay away from situations that might lead to a negative outcome. Tell them you'll pray for their safety. They might ridicule you, but that's OK. Follow your conscience and listen to the Holy Spirit. Let them

know you have a God to answer to and invite them to church.

3. Show accountability: Hold yourself and your family and friends to a higher standard. Form a small group of friends who have the same goal but have different ideas for achieving it. It's always good to get diverse feedback from people with different viewpoints. Talk and pray together and help each other along the way.

4. Enforce the rules: As a parent, hold strong to your house-hold rules. If you tell your kids to be home at a certain time and they are late, then administer a penalty that will discourage them from doing it again, such as grounding them from using the car or taking away their phone for a day. There is a difference between being a leader and being a dictator. Show love but enforce any rule that you feel is necessary and teach your children that disobedi-ence has consequences. "Owe no one anything, except to love each other, for the one who loves another has fulfilled the law" (Romans 13:8 ESV).

5. Forgive: Tough love means you show forgiveness to a loved one who has wronged you. This might be hard, but it will pave the way for a better and more godly relationship. You may not always get an apology but showing mercy will give you freedom and a good night's rest. "You shall not take vengeance or bear a grudge against the sons of your own people, but you shall love your neighbor as yourself: I am the LORD" (Leviticus 19:18 ESV).

Tough Love

Bobby Bowden used the blowout to teach his son a lesson. He learned the hard way that winners will never hand a victory over to the opposition. It must be earned. Tommy Bowden used that experience to rebuild the Clemson program. He did not like losing, but he appreciated the message from his father. When you show tough love to a friend or family member that could lead them to freedom in Christ, they may or may not take your advice. But your conscience will be clear that you did all you could to love them and show them the way to a better life. God is on your side.

IRON STREAM MEDIA

If you enjoyed this book, will you consider sharing the message with others?

Let us know your thoughts. You can let the author know by visiting or sharing a photo of the cover on our social media pages or leaving a review at a retailer's site. All of it helps us get the message out!

Email: info@ironstreammedia.com

@ironstreammedia

Brookstone Publishing Group, Iron Stream, Iron Stream Fiction, Iron Stream Harambee, Iron Stream Kids, and Life Bible Study are imprints of Iron Stream Media, which derives its name from Proverbs 27:17, "As iron sharpens iron, so one person sharpens another." This sharpening describes the process of discipleship, one to another. With this in mind, Iron Stream Media provides a variety of solutions for churches, ministry leaders, and nonprofits ranging from in-depth Bible study curriculum and Christian book publishing to custom publishing and consultative services.

For more information on ISM and its imprints, please visit IronStreamMedia.com

BROOKSTONE
PUBLISHING GROUP

IRON STREAM

IRON STREAM FICTION

IRON STREAM HARAMBEE PRESS

IRON STREAM KIDS

life
Bible Study

www.ingramcontent.com/pod-product-compliance
Lightning Source LLC
Chambersburg PA
CBHW062104080426
42734CB00012B/2742